THE TAROT OF

Enchanted Dreams

YASMEEN WESTWOOD

REDFeather™

MIND | BODY | SPIRIT

4880 Lower Valley Road, Atglen, PA 19310

Library of Congress Control Number: 2019936855

Designed by Brenda McCallum
Type set in Desire/Minion

ISBN: 978-0-7643-5828-9
Printed in China

Published by Red Feather Mind, Body, Spirit
An imprint of Schiffer Publishing, Ltd.
4880 Lower Valley Road | Atglen, PA 19310
Phone: (610) 593-1777; Fax: (610) 593-2002
E-mail: Info@schifferbooks.com
Web: www.redfeathermbs.com

For our complete selection of fine books on this and related subjects, please visit our website at www.schifferbooks.com. You may also write for a free catalog.

Schiffer Publishing's titles are available at special discounts for bulk purchases for sales promotions or premiums. Special editions, including personalized covers, corporate imprints, and excerpts, can be created in large quantities for special needs. For more information, contact the publisher.

We are always looking for people to write books on new and related subjects. If you have an idea for a book, please contact us at proposals@schifferbooks.com.

This deck is dedicated to all those who sat in their classrooms daydreaming of magical lands.

Welcome to my world.

Contents

Welcome 7

Introduction 8

The Major Arcana Explanation 12
The Minor Arcana Explanation 14
The Court Cards Explanation 16
Beginning a Reading 18
Learning the Cards 20
Basic Tarot Spreads 21
3-Card Spread 21
4-Card Love Spread 22
5-Card Spread 23
7-Card Relationship Spread 24
10-Card Celtic Cross Spread 26
12-Card Astrological Spread 28
16-Card General Spread 30

The Major Arcana 32
The Suit of Cups 78
The Suit of Swords 94
The Suit of Wands 110
The Suit of Pentacles 126

Acknowledgments 142

Welcome

Welcome to *The Tarot of Enchanted Dreams* and the guidebook on how to understand and read the Tarot cards. Tarot has been gaining in popularity over the years, as more and more people look toward personal self-development and are more open to exploring the unseen. Being a Tarot reader no longer carries the negative connotations it did in the past.

The purpose of this guidebook, apart from explaining the meanings of each card, is to help you use Tarot as a tool for self-development, to help you understand yourself better. Tarot works by tapping into your intuition, a very powerful inner voice, which if you listen to it can help you with life decisions and also assist in times of uncertainty. We ALL have the power to access this intuition. No special powers or abilities are required to do so. The Tarot is a tool to help you find and utilize this inner voice.

The guidebook has been written in a format that will allow you to journal as you work through the cards. Each card contains a question for you to ponder, as well as an affirmation and a task to do relating to the card. So, the more honest you are in answering the questions, the more you will begin to find out who you are, and using the cards daily will help sharpen your intuition until you are able to recognize and listen to it without having to try.

For me, Tarot is like a dreamworld, a place where magic happens, and I am so excited to bring this dreamworld to you. Creating this deck has been and is a wonderful journey involving a lot of fun (and tears), and with each card I have put in a little bit of myself. So welcome to *The Tarot of Enchanted Dreams* . . . let the magic begin!

Lots of Love,
Yasmeen xx

Introduction

What Is the Tarot?

Tarot cards have been around since the fourteenth century and appear to have originated in Europe. The oldest surviving set is called the Tarocchi in Italian and appears to date from 1420 to 1450. Some people believe they originated in ancient Egypt, and the common myth is that Tarot was brought to Europe by gypsies.

Tarot cards have frequently been used as a tool for fortune telling or divination and have been used in one form or another for understanding the self and the world. So, it's no wonder that in this time of chaos in the world, Tarot seems to be growing in popularity!

In the past, and even now, people who interpreted the cards were given great power and held in reverence as great fortune tellers, and this seems to be the case today, with people believing the interpretation as "the truth" as exactly what is going to happen and that nothing can be done to change it. However, I believe that little in our lives is fixed, and we can influence and change most things in our lives—but only if we choose to take responsibility for our own lives.

Misconceptions of Tarot?

Unfortunately, there are some people who seem to have a negative view of the Tarot cards; they think they are the work of the devil or some sort of black magic. People assume that if you can read the Tarot, then it means you can delve deep into their minds and know all their deepest and darkest secrets! That is definitely not the case. There are, however, other misconceptions made about the Tarot by people who have never used it:

1. Tarot can tell you EVERYTHING! The Tarot does not tell you 100 percent categorically what is going to happen in your life; only YOU have complete control over what happens in your life. The Tarot cannot tell you what decisions to make; it can help you look at things you may not have considered. But at the end of the day, you are the one who can make the choice and feel the consequences arising from it. You cannot blame the Tarot if the outcome is not what you expected, based upon a decision YOU made. Most importantly (and this scare loads of people), the Tarot is very unlikely to predict death.

2. Tarot is something to fear! There is nothing to fear with Tarot. It is made up of picture cards, which are open to YOUR interpretation. Someone else may look at the exact same image and interpret it in a totally different way. Also, you may look at the same card another day and see something entirely different. Tarot is not associated with any religion, cult, devil, voodoo, or any other sinister thing.

3. Tarot requires psychic skills! Not true. You do not have to have any special skills nor do you need to be a clairvoyant, medium, or psychic to be able to work with the cards. Anyone can "read" the cards. All you are doing is telling a story based on what the images show. We all possess natural psychic skills, and sometimes using the cards on a daily basis can open up these skills.

These are just a few of the misconceptions people have of Tarot. Are there any other misconceptions or rules you've heard of? What are they?

Choosing a Tarot Deck

Many people ask me how to choose a Tarot deck. Well, what I do is look at new decks that are available on Amazon, Google, or other venues. These sites always have images of decks, and I look at what imagery "speaks" to me. Some decks resonate very strongly while others do not at all. It's very important to look at decks, as you need the cards to be able to "talk" to you. I have found that when I love the imagery, then it's very easy to interpret the cards rather than struggle with interpretation of cards whose images you really do not like.

Storing Tarot Cards

Traditionally, Tarot cards are stored in a silk cloth—silk protects from negative energies. There are many ways in which you can protect your cards from negative energies and to ensure they are not damaged: a silk scarf, wooden box, tin box, cloth, etc.

Cleaning your Tarot Cards

Tarot cards need to be cleaned occasionally to remove any residual energies, especially when people have been shuffling and handling the cards a lot. This can be done in a number of ways. Again, choose what you feel comfortable with. I tend to cleanse my cards using incense. You can use

- smudging with sage and/or incense
- crystals
- Reiki

For more information about cleansing and other similar applications, one good resource is www.biddytarot.com.

Ethics of Reading

Know that you have responsibilities when you read for others. Readings must be done with the intention of helping the person who has come to you for a reading, NOT for enhancing your ego or for you to use that information in a negative way against a person. It is completely unethical and extremely irresponsible to predict anyone's death. NEVER EVER do that! If you see tough times ahead for someone, then it is best to talk about any problems or challenges ahead rather than a black-and-white reading.

Do NOT make decisions for another; by all means give advice and get them to see what they need to do, but do not offer any unsolicited advice, as it could come back and bite you!

Always remember to inform people that there is NO guarantee regarding any prediction and that they make their own choices. Do not play doctor, and never make a judgment or diagnosis about any ill health as you are not a medical practitioner.

Respect at all times the free will of every human, and keep yourself centered in love and light. Remember that we are all divine in essence. Do not judge; seek understanding.

How Can Tarot Help?

Tarot can do the following:

1. Help you tap into your own intuition and inner wisdom, so you can "know" with accuracy when something is right for you. It can also help validate your own feelings as to what the next steps are for you.

2. Help you see light at the end of the tunnel when you are surrounded in darkness and life feels hopeless. The Tarot may help by bringing in hope, optimism, and encouragement to your life. Sometimes that is enough to open up to your own creativity, problem solving, and intuition, and the ability to notice a different way forward.

3. Help you if you have a difficult choice to make, by helping you safely explore various options before you rush in and commit yourself to something that you may later regret.

4. Help by showing you the energies around you and indicate what may be blocking you from having the success you deserve or from moving forward. Often the Tarot can assist to show you the ways to overcome the blocks, by asking you probing questions.

What other ways do you think the Tarot can help?

The Major Arcana
EXPLANATION

A standard Tarot deck consists of 78 cards divided into two parts: the Major and Minor Arcana. There are 22 cards in the Major Arcana, from The Fool (0) to The World (XXI or 21). There are 56 cards in the Minor Arcana, divided into 4 Suits. For each suit, the cards are numbered Ace to Ten, and there are 4 Court Cards (Page, Knight, Queen, and King). These 22 cards of the Major Arcana symbolize some universal aspect of human experience.

If you see a lot of Major Arcana cards in a reading or a spread, then it is likely that those issues are very important issues in the person's life and that the impact of the situations may well be there for some time. They cover virtually every aspect of someone's life. It can also be seen as the journey through life or a more spiritual journey, and the lessons that need to be learned, as they point to some major lessons or qualities we need to find in ourselves to be able to move forward with a situation and often with our lives.

Some say that the Major Arcana shows the different stages on an individual's journey of inner growth—in what some call the Fool's Journey: a journey to self-realization, that we all travel through life, complete with detours, backups, and restarts.

The Minor Arcana
EXPLANATION

The rest of the deck is made up of four suits, called the Minor Arcana, representing the day-to-day nature of life. These can be compared to the suits in a deck of playing cards.

The first is the **Suit of Cups**, which usually represents emotions and feelings, the dreamy, emotional aspects of our life, and has to do with relationships. So, we have the beginning of a relationship (Ace of Cups) all the way to the happy family (Ten of Cups). Astrologically they represent the element of Water and the signs of Cancer, Scorpio, and Pisces.

The next is the **Suit of Wands**: our creativity, ambitions, and decisions in the world. The Wands refer to matters to do with action, work, career, business, creativity, moving forward. Wands are represented by the element of Fire and represent the zodiac signs of Aries, Leo, and Sagittarius.

Then we have the **Suit of Swords**, which are the Suit of the Mind: our thoughts, our worries, our concerns, and matters of knowledge, and they point toward mental activity and head stuff with thoughts, ideas, fears, and logic. Swords represent the element Air and the astrological signs of Gemini, Libra, and Aquarius.

Last, we have the Suit of Pentacles, which are all about the material things in life, be it money, resources, or your time. They show us all the different stages of financial issues. Pentacles represent the element of Earth and the astrological signs of Taurus, Virgo, and Capricorn.

The Court Cards
EXPLANATION

The Court Cards can indicate people with certain character traits, as well as emotions that people may experience.

The Page. The Pages in a suit represent new beginnings or some message being offered to you—something with the potential to change you.

The Knight. The Knights are all about action and bravery. They are also known for their impulsiveness and about *doing* something as opposed to waiting for something to happen *to* you.

Page of Cups

Knight of Wands

The Queen. The Queen in a suit is about nurturing, compassion, intuition, and protection. The Queen has mastered the traits of the suit in which she is found.

The King. The King is all about success, control, mastery, wisdom, and fairness. The King shows the characteristics of maturity of its suit and, like the Queen, has mastered all there is to know about the suit, and as such can use his wisdom to counsel others.

Beginning a Reading

Step 1: Set the mood
The first step is to relax your mind and to ground yourself. So, make yourself comfortable, listen to meditative music, or burn incense. I tend to burn incense to help me open up my intuition and imagine roots coming out of my feet, going deep into the ground, to help me ground, as I can find I get quite "spacey" otherwise. Clear your mind, and release any tension your body, because if you are tense, then you will not be relaxed enough to do the reading.

Step 2: Shuffle the cards
You need to shuffle your cards as they may still be in the previous reading order. To ensure you are starting with a clear deck, shuffle your cards, imagining clear light bathing the cards. It is important to shuffle the cards because this is how you sort through all the forms your reading could take, and arrange at a subtle level the card you will receive.

Step 3: Ask the question
Holding your deck, ask the question in your head. How you ask the question is important. A reading may be completely general, directed toward a particular area of concern or performed to address a specific question. Instead of a type of question with a clear yes or no answer, consider asking what you need to know from the cards regarding a particular situation, or what the message for the day is.

Step 4: Select your cards
One way to choose is to place your Tarot deck in front of you and, using your left hand, cut the deck in half and place the top half on the left. You should have two piles of cards now. Choose the card that is on the top of the right pile, and turn it over. This is just a guide, and you may have your own way of selecting cards. I do not cut the deck. Whenever I shuffle, cards tend to jump out, and those are the ones that I select. There is no right or wrong way in which to select your cards.

Step 5: Create the spread

A spread is a pattern for laying out the cards. It defines how many cards to use, where each one goes, and what each one means. A spread is a template guiding the placement of the cards so they can shed light on a given topic. There are many, many different types of spreads, and some of the more common ones are listed in the forthcoming pages. Choose your cards as per the shuffling technique in step 4 and lay them out in front of you as per the spread chosen. Pick all cards before turning them over for an interpretation.

Step 6: Interpret the reading

For the actual reading you may want to keep a pen and paper handy to record what comes up during the reading, or to record it as a voice clip. Do not censor what comes up—be honest and let it flow. These are the things to look out for:

- What is the name of the card?
- Describe the card; what do you see on it? It may be literal or your impression. What is going on in the card? Is it an action card or a card where nothing much is happening? Who is in the card? Why do you think they are there?
- What are the symbols on the card? Describe the image, colors, numbers, or words that catch your attention. What do the colors mean to you? What do the symbols mean?
- What is the mood of the card? How does this card make you feel? Do you like the feeling of it, or does the mood make you want to put it away?
- What does this card make you think of? Does it remind you of an event or someone from your life? Notice your first impressions and your emotional reaction to it. Why do you think you have had that emotional reaction?
- What else stands out?
- If you were in the card, what story would it be telling you?

Step 7: Closing the reading

When you feel it is time to end the Tarot reading, write down the cards you selected and their positions. It is easy to forget them—especially if you have a memory like mine! Then, clear the deck to remove all traces of the energy patterns of this reading; this can be done by scrambling the cards together gently.

Before putting the cards away, hold your deck in your hands and silently thank it for all the insights and guidance it has brought to you this day. Express your gratitude to your Inner Guide for helping you via the Tarot cards.

Learning the Cards

Keeping a Tarot Journal

A Tarot journal is a place where you can record your personal thoughts, insights, observations, and notes about each of the cards to help expand your Tarot knowledge and skills. The journal can also include Tarot readings that you have done, spreads you have used or created, and your own notes about each card. The journal can be either a notebook you have personalized or have created as an electronic format, or any medium that you feel comfortable with.

Perhaps one of the most common methods for learning the cards with a Tarot journal is to use the Card-a-Day exercise, where you can use your journal to record your thoughts on an individual Tarot card drawn for each day. That is what I used to do when I was learning about the decks rather than trying to remember every single card in one go. Capture the aspects we looked at above, and you will find that you form your own meanings for each of the cards. Each card will mean something to YOU. Assign people you know with the characteristics of the card as it makes it easier to remember. I've done that and found it to be quite fun! Don't be surprised if you can't remember all of them straight away. Learn the keywords associated with each card—if you like—and it can be helpful to imagine each card as a character in a story . . . What story would it tell you? Note this in your journal.

The more you use your cards, the quicker you will learn, and they will become familiar to you. And you may find that they begin to talk to you as soon as you pick them up!

Basic Tarot Spreads

The following are basic Tarot spreads to help you begin your Tarot journey. As you become more and more familiar with the different spreads, you may consider adjusting these or consider creating your own spreads.

1. 3-Card Spread
2. Love Tarot Spread (4 cards)
3. 5-Card Spread
4. 7-Card Relationship Spread
5. 10-Card Celtic Cross Spread
6. 12-Card Astrological Spread
7. 16-Card General Spread

3-CARD SPREAD

This 3-card Tarot spread is a quick and simple way to get insight into the past, present, and future. If you need clarification on any of the positions and meanings, you can always draw an extra card.

4-CARD LOVE SPREAD

This is a good spread to use if you are looking for insight into a romantic relationship. You can use it to check out your physical, mental, and spiritual/emotional connections with your other half.

Card 1: Physical connection

The physical (sex and intimacy; physical attraction)

Card 2: Mental connection

Similar interests and communication

Card 3: Spiritual/emotional connection

Shared goals, dreams, and love; mutual respect for each other

Card 4: Long-term potential of relationship

5-CARD SPREAD

The 5-card Tarot spread gives a quick answer or answers to some very basic problems and concerns. The spread can be repeated multiple times to represent different facets of a problem.

Card 1: Present position

How have you arrived at the point you are now?

Card 2: Present expectations

What are your expectations now?

Card 3: The unexpected

What is being hidden from you at the moment but may happen?

Card 4: Immediate future

What will be arriving shortly
(it could be people, events etc.)?

Card 5: Long-term future

What is the long-term future?

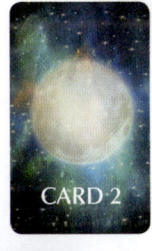

7-CARD RELATIONSHIP SPREAD

This spread can give you some important insight into the inner workings of your relationship, including challenges, hopes, dreams, needs, and wants, guiding you toward deeper communication and understanding.

Card 1: Your personality

Card 2: Partner's personality

Card 3: Your challenges/blocks (challenges you bring into relationship)

Card 4: Partner's challenges/blocks (challenges they bring into relationship)

Card 5: Your hopes and dreams

Card 6: Partners hopes and dreams

Card 7: What connects you? (What is it that brings you together?)

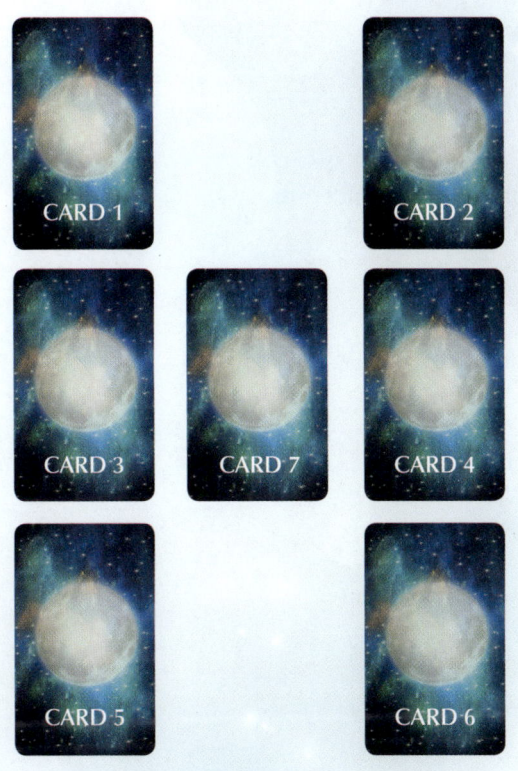

10-CARD CELTIC CROSS SPREAD

The 10-card Celtic Cross spread is the most commonly used layout for reading the cards. It gives an overview of the past, present, and future. There are many different versions of the Celtic Cross spread, so please feel free to add your twist to it if you wish.

Card 1: Situation now

Card 2: What's helping/hindering

Card 3: Subconscious influence

Card 4: Past

Card 5: Conscious desires

Card 6: Immediate future

Card 7: How you see yourself

Card 8: How others see you

Card 9: Hopes/fears

Card 10: Final outcome

12-CARD ASTROLOGICAL SPREAD

This spread can also be used to represent the 12 houses of a person's life in astrology. It is useful to gain more information into a particular area. Again, you can add more cards to each house for more detail.

What is a House? You may have seen a birth chart and wondered why it looks like a pizza cut into 12 slices.

The houses refer to different areas of the sky, and astrologically there are 12 houses in a birth chart; each symbolizes 12 categories of life where the action of your life takes place, or challenges that you may face along the way. The first house is always located at the position where the hour hand is at nine o'clock on the face of a clock. The rest of the houses are lined up going in a counterclockwise direction on the zodiac wheel.

Understanding the houses of the chart can help you understand where you are comfortable, where you find challenge, and where the dramas of your life take place.

House 1: The self (our personality and how others see us)

House 2: Money and possessions

House 3: Communication as well as day-to-day activities

House 4: Home life, ancestry, siblings, family, parents

House 5: Pleasure, romance, parties, children, affairs, creativity

House 6: Work and health, both emotional and physical

House 7: Partnerships, both personal and professional, marriage

House 8: Legacies, the occult, sex, death, transformations

House 9: Spiritual, religion, education, travel, philosophy

House 10: Career, profession, authority, fame, reputation

House 11: Friends, groups, organizations, hopes, and dreams

House 12: Fears, enemies, the unseen, subconscious, restrictions, dangers

16-CARD GENERAL SPREAD

This 16-card general spread gives us a good overall impression of what's going on with a person physically, emotionally, mentally, and spiritually. It shows us the potential for the next 12 months and highlights any problem areas that may need addressing. I love this spread and have used it many, many times!

Cards 1 and 2: The past and how it affects what is going on now

Cards 3 and 4: The present

Cards 5 and 6: What the person desires

Card 7: Focus area

Card 8: What needs to be avoided

Cards 9 and 10: Next 3 months

Cards 11 and 12: Next 3–6 months

Cards 13 and 14: Next 6–9 months

Cards 15 and 16: Next 9–12 months

The Major Arcana

0
The Fool

I
The Magician

II
The High Priestess

III
The Empress

IV
The Emperor

V
The Guide

VI
The Lovers

VII
The Chariot

VIII
Strength

IX
The Hermit

The Fool

"Come to the edge," he said.
We can't, we're afraid!" they responded. Come to the edge," he said. We
can't, we will fall!" they responded. Come to the edge," he said. And so
they came. And he pushed them . . . and they flew."

~Guillaume Apollinaire

Keywords: New beginnings, optimism, trust in life, new ideas, childlike ambitions, carefree, go with the flow, trust yourself, heading into the unknown, simplicity, a new adventure, leap of faith, personal quest, potential of spirit, courage

Meaning: The Fool card in a reading may represent an opportunity for new beginnings. It's about taking the leap of faith with no idea where we are going, but to go anyway. Are you apprehensive of someone or something? Trust in the Universe and let go of any fears. Just know that this journey will change you, and many lessons will be learned along the way! A journey of a thousand steps begins with taking the first step, no matter how daunting the journey may seem. The Fool card denotes the beginning of a new life cycle. It also could exhibit naivety or innocence. Something new and unpredictable may be about to cross your path. So, what do you fear? Go to the edge and fly!

Question: If you could start anything, knowing it would reach success, what would you do?

Affirmation: "Today I say yes to a new adventure."

Task: Start something new today. What will it be?

I
The Magician

I
The Magician

"Magic is believing in yourself;
if you can do that, you can make anything happen."
~Johann Wolfgang von Goethe

Keywords: Action, the power to manifest, inner abilities, manifesting, creating, mastery and skill, directing will with confidence, concentration, alchemy, resourcefulness, mastery over thoughts

Meaning: Use and trust your intuition. Then act. You probably have far more internal resources than you give yourself credit for. Everything that you need to manifest your desires is within you. You have all the tools, but you have to ensure that you are focusing the power and will of the mind on what you DO want. Your thoughts can create your reality. Become aware of your own self and the power within you. Pay attention to your internal chatter. Is it negative or positive? This card may be a person whom you know or who is coming into your life. He may be someone who is self-assured, knows his own worth, and is coming into your life to help you create what it is that you desire. You are advised to look closer at something that may appear too good to be true, as this card can indicate all is not what it seems to be. It may be a person or a job. Do your homework now so you do not have regret later.

Question: Where do you focus your energies?

Affirmation: "I have the power to manifest anything I desire."

Task: Gather old magazines or use the internet to print off images of your desires and create a vision board. Place the board where you can see it every day.

II
The High Priestess

"Intuition is seeing with the soul."
~Dean Koontz

Keywords: Intuition, clairvoyance, premonition, perceptivity, going within, hidden secrets, unconscious awareness, potential, trusting inner wisdom

Meaning: Trust your intuition; tap into your inner guidance system through relaxation and meditation. You may have to ask probing questions to get all the information you need. You might only discover the right questions to ask through meditation or by paying attention to your dreams. You may need to hold certain information that you have close to your chest, for now is not the right time to share. Are you in a situation or at a crossroads and don't know what to do? Listen to your gut feeling; what does it say? Our intuition always has the answers we seek if only we can quiet the mind to listen. Some things are currently hidden to you; something is going on below the surface, and you need to listen to your intuition and pay close attention to what your "gut feelings" are telling you about a situation. Do not make any decisions at this time, as you do not have all the facts. All will be revealed soon and provide you with an understanding of your situation. Be patient.

Question: Do you have the courage to trust yourself and your instincts?

Affirmation: "I invite guidance and clarity."

Task: Today, pay attention to the world around you. Look out for any signs or synchronicities and what they are telling you.

III
The Empress

III
The Empress

*"You carry Mother Earth within you. She is not outside you.
Mother Earth is not just your environment."*

~Nhat Hanh

Keywords: Harvest, natural growth, abundance, fertility, pregnancy, motherhood, nature, nurturing, creativity, sensuality, unconditional love

Meaning: This card represents femininity and motherhood. There is abundance, joy, passion, and flow in life generally. You may be birthing a new, creative venture or dream. Keep nurturing those ideas as they will grow into a rich harvest of abundance and success. You will have to spend a lot of time and energy to make this a success, in the same way a child comes into the world—moving from conception to birth. It does not happen overnight. This is a very positive card of growth and abundance. There is balance and harmony and a feeling of nurturing, whether that is for you or from someone else. This is an excellent card with regard to fertility matters and can represent pregnancy or birth. The Empress brings comfort, love, protection, and understanding to the people she loves. Allow yourself to be sensitive and compassionate with yourself and others around you.

Questions: What would you like to create and birth into this world, and how will you go about doing it?

Affirmation: "I deserve to love and pamper myself, because when I love myself, I love others."

Task: Celebrate motherhood today. Create a time capsule for your children to be opened on a certain date. Make it unique and fun!

IV
The Emperor

IV
The Emperor

"If your actions inspire others to dream more, learn more, do more, and become more, then you are a leader."

~John Adams

Keywords: Control, dominance, energy, structure, stability, rules and power, fatherhood, authority, regulations, leadership, protection

Meaning: The Emperor represents external power, strength, and presence without a need to be showy—someone with a strong personal code of honor, who would do whatever it takes to protect his family and ensure that they are provided for. This is someone to whom rules, discipline, and structure are very important and are rigorously imposed on everyone else. If you are lacking in structure and discipline, this means to take control and apply rules and regulations to areas of your life. You are being asked to look at how you use power, as it can be very easy to misuse it and force others to bend to your way of working. There is controlling out of fear and controlling out of love. Look very carefully at how you are coming across to others. Do you allow people to voice their opinions, or do you think your way is the right way? Allow others to be who they are. If something in your life is out of control, use the traits of The Emperor to regain it.

Question: Where in your life are you lacking rules and structure?

Affirmation: "I assert healthy boundaries with respect and gentleness."

Task: Look at where you need to be more like The Emperor.

V

The Guide

V
The Guide

"Let the inner God that is in each one of us speak.
The temple is your body, and the priest is your heart; it is from here
that every awareness must begin."

~Alejandro Jodorowsky

Keywords: Knowledge, teacher, mentor, religious institutions, advice, wisdom, revelation, honoring rituals and ceremonies, conformity, conservative

Meaning: This card indicates the need to look at your beliefs. What are they, and where have they come from? Are you following belief systems of others, or are they really yours? How true are you to yourself? This card indicates conformity, rules, and tradition, some of which may be outdated but are still being followed, because that's just how it's always been. You may need help to delve deep into the mysteries of the Universe. Maybe you are feeling the need to consider joining some form of structured learning group, as you have decided you want to follow a conventional path and the traditional values of culture or society. Is there a situation happening now that is due to your beliefs? Try changing how you think about it, and see what effect it has on the situation. A spiritual mentor may cross your path. The advice here is to listen to what they have to say, but keep an open mind, and only take what resonates with you. You do not have to believe everything you are told.

Question: What external guidance do you need at this point in time?

Affirmation: "I hold the keys for unraveling spiritual truths, which supports my journey as a seeker of the unknown."

Task: Read, with an open mind, a spiritual book that you normally would not read.

VI
The Lovers

"To be fully seen by somebody, then, and be loved anyhow—
this is a human offering that can border on miraculous."

~Elizabeth Gilbert

Keywords: Love, relationships, choice, passion, uniting, sexual attraction, intimacy, romance

Meaning: The Lovers indicates being in love and showing it to others, expression of passionate feelings, and bringing people together. You have a choice to make, and you may be presented with two different paths. It could be about a relationship (whether romantic, business, or friendship) or some sort of temptation in your path. Whatever it is about, you are facing an important decision that may change your life. Weigh the consequences of each choice before you make up your mind. There may be a new romance on the horizon. Just be careful you do not create unrealistic expectations for someone and start viewing them through rose-tinted glasses. Alternatively, you may have this image in your head of the "perfect" person, and you completely miss someone right under your nose. There may even be a choice of two lovers! Remember that there is no such thing as a perfect person. Make sure you are realistic. For couples, there may be a deepening of the bonds that already exist.

Questions: Do you have difficulty truly loving yourself? Why?

Affirmation: "I see the best in everyone and everything through the eyes of love and compassion."

Task: Today, take someone whom you do not get along with, and look at them through the love of your inner spirit. Can you see why they are the way they are?

VII
The Chariot

VII
The Chariot

"The Self is the rider in the Chariot
of the body, of which the senses are the horses and the mind, the reins."

~Bhagavad Gita

Keywords: Progress, integration, willpower, journey, balance, forward movement, force, ambition, control, resilience, self-determination

Meaning: The Chariot triumphs over obstacles and breaking through barriers. It's about being in control of where you are heading and fulfilling your goals through determination, self-discipline, and focus. This could indicate travel . . . a change of direction. Your life is in YOUR hands. It is now time to move forward with whatever you have been in the process of planning. It is an action card, and you cannot do any more planning. It's time . . . get going! No matter what happens, it's up to you to ensure you remain in control at all times, even at times when the way ahead is not clear. There is a need to focus and control your emotions, or you may find yourself being pulled in many directions, causing chaos. The Chariot can indicate being controlled by emotions, food, materialistic needs, work, or belief systems. Perhaps you are planning a road trip or considering purchasing a car.

Questions: Are you in control of your life, or have you handed it over to something else? What can you do to take it back?

Affirmation: "I invite guidance and clarity."

Task: Plan and go on a road trip.

VIII
Strength

VIII
Strength

"Opportunities to find deeper powers within ourselves come when life seems most challenging."

~Joseph Campbell

Keywords: Inner strength, power, energy, courage, and taking control of your life; gentleness with quiet determination, courage; and endurance, patience, compassion, soft control

Meaning: Strength is about the need to call on your inner courage, to have grace under pressure with the strength to endure. It's a time of quiet determination, to keep your head down and keep going. Deal with situations in a gentle, calm manner. At all times there lies within you a place of calmness and strength. Learn how to tap into it. You are being asked to work with your inner nature and not to let it take over. Do not allow fear, ego, or physical desires to become uncontrollable. You are paralyzed by a situation, and fear is stopping you from moving forward. You need to confront your fear and have courage to face it as you have more power than the fear. The fear exists only in your mind, where you have let it go wild and fierce so that it's taken over. Tame the wild beast within. YOU are the one in control, not your fear! Be strong, confident, and courageous!

Questions: Do you know where you want to go in life? Are you allowing fear to control what happens in your life? Is it stopping you from doing the things you desire?

Affirmation: "I am bold and brave and can face anything that confronts me."

Task: Do one thing today that terrifies you. How do you feel after doing it?

IX
The Hermit

IX
The Hermit

"Loneliness is the poverty of self; solitude is the richness of self."

~May Sarton

Keywords: Loneliness, perspective, solitude, inspiration, introspection, searching, guidance, stillness, withdrawal, time out, meditation

Meaning: The Hermit seeks answers by retreating or being in solitude. There is a need for some quiet time to reflect. Light the way for those less experienced. This card can suggest withdrawal for deep thought and contemplation, a time of quiet introspection to reflect and meditate in order to find the answer that lies within you. You need to withdraw from contact with the outside world for a period of time in order to remove yourself from any distractions that may be hampering your search for the answers to questions on your mind. You could be needing a time-out in a relationship to evaluate the future of it. It may be a temporary separation while you work things out. This is a time for soul searching and inner work. If you are an empath and take on other people's energies, you will need to shut yourself away from people for a while to recharge. Perhaps you are sick and stuck at home to recuperate. Just be careful that your solitude or hermit-like attitude is not you hiding from a situation, or that you are hiding away because you may be too proud to ask for help.

Question: How much time do you spend on your own?

Affirmation: "The answers I seek are within me."

Task: Today, find some time to be alone—away from electronic gadgets—and allow yourself to just be. Head out into nature if you can.

X

The Wheel of
Destiny

X
The Wheel of Destiny

"How people treat you is their karma; how you react is yours."

~Wayne Dyer

Keywords: Change in fortune, change of luck, destiny, karma, fate, opportunity, randomness, cycles, ups and downs, serendipity

Meaning: This card symbolizes the changing nature of life and its ups and downs. In life there will always be good and bad times, and no matter what you do, you cannot change that. Life is about just allowing events to unfold and trusting your luck. There could be unexpected events and a belief that what goes around comes around. A new cycle is beginning where luck is on your side, so make the most of the opportunities being presented. This card asks that you stop going on an emotional roller coaster when things happen that you don't like; sometimes s#*t just happens! Take it in your stride and accept it for what it is. We don't need to control or fix everything. If you have been going through some difficult times, then the message of the card is that things will change for the better, as no matter how dark the night, there is always a new dawn. So, if things are good just now, enjoy! If things are bad, it will not be forever.

Question: What seeds are you sowing for tomorrow?

Affirmation: "All the good I put out into the world will come back to me."

Task: Take any events that occur in your stride today, whether they are negative or positive. Just see them as an event and remain centered throughout.

XI
Justice

"There is a higher court than courts of justice, and that is the court of conscience. It supersedes all other courts."

~Gandhi

Keywords: Justice, responsibility, making decisions that are based on facts, cause and effect, balance, fairness, right, deserving, rule, law/legal matters, wisdom

Meaning: Justice is about making an objective decision based on facts—no place for emotion here. Consider all evidence and deliberate before concluding. You may be involved in legal matters either yourself or for/with someone else. Justice will be done in the situation, whether it is favorable or unfavorable for you. Be honest in legal matters; otherwise, one day or another it will come back to you. Look at where there is justice or injustice in your own life. You are where you are meant to be in life just now as a consequence of decisions you've made earlier on. There is a need to take full responsibility for whatever situation you are in right now. How did it come about? What choices did you make? Be really honest with yourself. You can lie to others, but can you really lie to yourself? How can you make amends?

Questions: What injustice might you be struggling with right now? Can you change it or understand it better?

Affirmation: "I shall not submit to injustice from anyone!"

Task: List a couple of decisions you can make today to bring more justice into your life.

XII
Perspective

*"If you change the way you look at things,
the things you look at change."*

~Wayne Dyer

Keywords: Suspension, life in limbo, alternative view, self-sacrifice, letting go, reversal, surrender, new perspective, enlightenment, grace, delays, reflection, insight

Meaning: You are in a time of change, a time to pause before you can move on. This card can be about delays, and there isn't much you can do about it. It is not the right time for what you want. You need to wait patiently and not act. Stop pushing and forcing things to happen, and let matters take their own natural course. Look for solutions through stillness and meditation, rather than being busy doing a hundred other things. There may be a need for a new perspective or to view something from the opposite direction. You certainly see the world very differently when you look at it upside down, so just be and observe. You could be in a period of transition right now—moving from one phase of life to another and feeling stuck. You need to look inside yourself and change the way you view things to see if there is something you are hung up about that is causing you to remain where you are.

Questions: Why are you feeling stuck or suspended at this time in your life? What is going on for you?

Affirmation: "I let go of what no longer serves me."

Task: Are you feeling stuck in limbo because your old ways have led you to this "stuckness"? List what you can shed to move on.

XIII
Death

"Just when the caterpillar thought its world was over,
it became a butterfly."

~Old proverb

Keywords: Endings, new beginnings, let go of old, transformation, change, transition, elimination, regeneration, renewal, rebirth

Meaning: A major change is upon you—if it is not already here. It is a transition from one stage to another. It could be that an unpleasant phase of life is coming to an end. Once this ending happens, there is no coming back. Like death, this ending is final. It could be something that has now served its purpose, and it's time to leave it. You may be leaving one way completely in order for a new way to come into existence. This card is about massive change and transformation, and while it may be difficult and painful, there is a necessary ending, as from an ending can grow new beginnings. Embrace the change. Do not try to resist it; otherwise it will cause you more grief than necessary. Know that death is always accompanied by a rebirth. The more you hold on and try to control the situation, the more uncomfortable you will be. Let go whatever is ending, so that you can make space for the beautiful things the Universe has waiting for you.

Question: What is already dead or in the process of dying that you are still holding on to?

Affirmation: "The divine within me is eternal."

Task: If you are struggling with depression over a loss, consider talking to someone. Seek professional help if you cannot speak to those close to you

XIV
Temperance

"Problems arise in that one has to find a balance between what people need from you and what you need for yourself."

~Jessye Norman

Keywords: Healing, renewal, emotional balance, calm, plenty, flow of life, serenity, testing the waters, keeping options open, peace, diplomacy, moderation

Meaning: There is a need to find balance, whether it's in the professional or personal life. Find a middle ground and use your ability to find compromise and balance. Are you feeling out of sync? Maybe you are giving too much time to work and not enough to your home life—or vice versa. Your life needs readjusting to ensure a healthy mind and body. If you are not balanced, then you may find your energy being scattered in many different directions, and as a result, you could end up with an illness. Everything needs to be in moderation: emotions, food, work, etc. Take the time to listen to and feel your emotions to sense if you are in a harmonious state. We have within us the power to remain balanced no matter what life throws at us. It could be something as simple as making sure you are drinking enough water.

Question: What can you do today to bring more balance into your life?

Affirmation: "I create harmony in my life by maintaining a balanced lifestyle."

Task: Consider looking at which parts of your life could do with being balanced. Do you spend too much time watching TV or on the internet, for example?

XV
The Devil

XV
The Devil

"No one can make you feel inferior without your consent."

~Eleanor Roosevelt

Keywords: Bondage, materialism, ignorance, hopelessness, attachment, addiction, narcissism, ego, obsession, manipulation, secrets, darkness, giving away power, destructive patterns/habits

Meaning: The Devil suggests hedonistic tendencies, the enjoyment of food, drink, sex, and material pleasures. But it often suggests overindulgence or excessive behavior, such as addictions to things that are unhealthy. It also indicates the need to deal with unhealthf impulses in a healthy way. You may be feeling trapped, but you can choose to free yourself whenever you wish, as the traps have been constructed by you. Someone may have addictive, manipulative, or abusive behaviors. Things are not necessarily what they appear to be, and you may be tricked into believing others, thus giving your power away instead of trusting yourself. Are you feeling bound to something or someone? Do you need to break free of the chains binding you, or perhaps you are so used to the chains that you are afraid to break free? How will you cope, as isn't it a case of "better the devil you know"? Is your mind playing tricks on you, trapping you in a state of false illusion, creating monsters? Confront your demons and take back your power. The only thing stopping you is fear.

Question: Whom or what are you giving your power away to?

Affirmation: "I release the victim mentality and take responsibility for every area of my life."

Task: Notice when you blame others for making you feel inferior. What can you do to be aware when you are doing this?

XVI
The Tower

XVI
The Tower

"It's a good thing to have all the props pulled out from under us occasionally. It gives us some sense of what is rock under our feet, and what is sand."

~Madeleine L'Engle

Keywords: Shock, sudden change, disgrace, calamity clearing away, release, downfall, sudden flash of insight, revelation, upheaval, unexpected event, freedom

Meaning: Something unexpected and unplanned is about to occur, and it will be causing major changes and considerable upheaval. It will sweep away what needs to change and make way for new and better things. It may be here, or you have had warnings for a while but have not done anything about it. You cannot control or fight it. The Tower will sweep away anything that is no longer required, whether you like it or not. It will break through any false illusions you had, leaving you with no option but to let go and move forward. It is a necessary destruction, one that will leave you shocked and numb. Whatever is destroyed was not built on solid foundations. Once you have gotten over the shock, you will need to regroup and build something with a stronger foundation—something that will not be knocked down in such a drastic way again. You may have created walls around you where you feel safe, maybe due to past hurts.

Questions: Do you feel as if life is falling apart? What false beliefs are being destroyed in the process?

Affirmation: "I invite guidance and clarity."

Task: Think of a time when the Tower came into your life. What was swept away, and what lessons did you learn?

XVII
The Star

XVII
The Star

*"Reach high, for the stars lie hidden in your soul.
Dream deep, for every dream precedes the goal."*

~Pamela Vaull Starr

Keywords: Renewal, hope, guidance, seeking a direction, inspiration, generosity, serenity, calm, wishes, dreams, travel, good fortune, healing, miracles

Meaning: The Star is a card of hope. It denotes calm and peace after the upheavals of The Tower. It is a message to you that the destruction was necessary, and now healing can take place. Dare to believe that you will rebuild and that what you now desire will happen. This card is giving you the gift of hope, and all we need is a tiny bit of that to achieve our desires. In tough times, hope is what keeps you going. Whatever tough times you may have gone through, there is now light at the end of the tunnel, and you are moving into better conditions. Though you may not see it, something beautiful is going to come out of whatever heartache or loss you have had to endure or are enduring, as healing, happiness, and your dreams are available to you. Bring back that faith you lost due to recent events. All will be well. We all have a light within us, ready to shine. So what are you waiting for? Go forth and shine!

Question: What gives me hope now?

Affirmation: "Today, and every day, I unleash my inner sparkle."

Task: Ask the Universe for something, and then let it go. Trust it will provide.

XVIII
The Moon

XVIII
The Moon

*"One does not become enlightened by naively 'imagining'
images of light, but by making the mind's darkness conscious."*

~Carl Jung

Keywords: Mystery, subconscious, dreams, reflection, uncertainty and fluctuating emotions, secrecy, illusion, fear, imagination, hidden emotions, paranoia, obsession

Meaning: You may be going through some very deep emotions right now due to uncertainty in your environment. It is your fear of the unknown that is the cause of this. By the light of the moon, nothing may appear as it really is, creating illusionary situations, so it's best not to jump to conclusions or believe anything until you have more information. Some facts are hidden from you, and they will be revealed to you over time. Wait until all the facts are available before making any decisions. It could be that a person is making themselves out to be something they are not, or even that you are so emotional that you are not allowing yourself to think rationally and are imagining monsters where there are none. Are you hiding or repressing memories/emotions? You need to bring them out to the light of the day and face them. This card can also indicate intuition, psychic matters and dreams, possible deceit and misunderstandings, or maybe a need to clarify matters, especially in communication. Pay attention to dreams and other signs that may cross your path. Do they have a message?

Question: Do you trust yourself and your instincts?

Affirmation: "I use my intuition to help guide me and my needs."

Task: Consider keeping a dream journal, and record your dreams as soon as you wake up. Is there a pattern? What is your subconscious trying to tell you?

XIX
The Sun

XIX
The Sun

"Turn your face to the sun, and the shadows fall behind you."

~Maori saying

Keywords: Love, celebration, creativity, health, happiness, joy, balance, youthfulness, health, vitality, success, attainment, glory, contentment, fame, fortune

Meaning: Happiness, hope, prosperity, and great fortune are indicated. Relationships are filled with happiness and contentment, career matters are successful, and health has energy and vitality. You will be feeling a sense of completeness and utter happiness, so much so that others will be able to sunbathe in the glow coming off you! You are seeing things clearly and experiencing intense joy. You could be gaining recognition for your work. Everything is coming up roses. Focus on all the joy and happiness in your life right now. Consider using this time to manifest your heart's desire. If you are feeling burned out, consider delegating or saying no! You may be planning your summer holidays to a hot destination, or even feel in the mood for an adventure and could think about booking a safari trip. Whatever it is, be happy just now. You deserve it!

Question: What am I grateful for today that I can celebrate?

Affirmation: "I shine my inner light bright, surrounding myself and others."

Task: Today, choose to approach the day filled with joy, no matter what happens. Smile at everyone you meet, and notice what happens.

XX
Judgment

XX
Judgment

*"A single event can awaken within us a stranger
totally unknown to us. To live is to be slowly born."*

~Antoine de Saint-Exupéry

Keywords: Judgment, rebirth, new phase, epiphany, awakening, resurrection, revival, inner calling, transformation, purpose

Meaning: Take a long, hard look at yourself. What are you hiding from yourself? You need to stop your negative thinking and step up to your full potential. You may be receiving a wake-up call or discovering a new purpose in life. You could be welcoming the start of a new phase of life or resurrecting something from the past. There is a feeling of cleansing the mistakes of the past and starting again with renewed hope. Examine your thoughts and behaviors to see if they are aligned to who you want to be. Learn from your mistakes and move on. Finally, you are on the right road. There can also be a sense of karma, in reaping what you have previously sown. Do not let this opportunity pass you by. Things may be happening faster, with karma being instantaneous as compared to The Wheel of Destiny card. What you put out will come back to you manyfold, so be very careful of what you say and do.

Questions: Do you allow others the space to be themselves, or do you try to mold them to how you think they should be?

Affirmation: "I accept myself for who I am without fear of judgment or criticism."

Task: Do something today that you normally would not do for fear of what others might think of you.

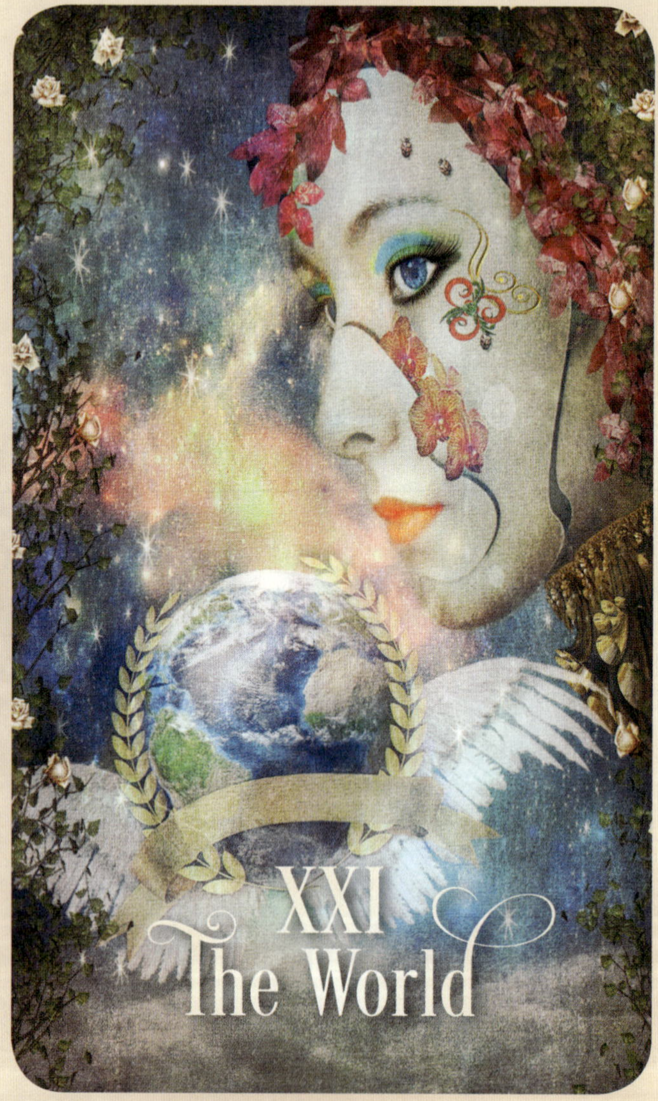
XXI
The World

XXI
The World

"Life is like riding a bicycle. To keep your balance,
you must keep moving."

~Albert Einstein

Keywords: Integration, accomplishment, completion, wholeness, attainment, success with fulfilment, triumph, end of a cycle, world at your feet

Meaning: You want it all! You want material, spiritual, and emotional stability. You are ready for a new cycle to begin. You love change, new experiences, meeting new people, adventure, and travel. You love the exotic, faraway places and may be planning a trip in a far-off destination. You have brought to fruition the results of your hard efforts. It is the end of a personal cycle or a project. Fulfilment and contentment, a feeling of having the world at your feet, having your dreams come true, having peace of mind, finding contentment, counting your blessings, a successful outcome, and things moving forward into a new cycle are all possible. The World indicates the end of a cycle and the beginning of a new one. You may be afraid of change and of the unknown. Have you fully closed the door on the previous or are there aspects from what has gone that you are still holding on to? Perhaps the old was comforting as it was known. However, it has ended, and now it's time to begin anew. What new adventures await? The world is your oyster and waiting for you to discover it!

Question: What sort of world have you been creating for yourself and others?

Affirmation: "I am a unique and special child of this world."

Task: Reflect on your journey so far, on a phase of your life. How have you arrived at where you are today, and what lessons have you learned?

The Suit of Cups

 Ace of Cups

*"You have to fill your cup.
You then give away the overflowing,
but you keep a cupful for yourself."*

~Wynonna Judd

Keywords: Overflowing, abundance, joy, happiness, new romance or friendship, new creativity, love, renewal

Meaning: The Ace of Cups marks the beginning of a new emotion. A new friendship or love may be offered to you, or a new project is beginning, one that will make use of your creative skills. There is also the chance of a new opportunity being presented to you that will make you feel very happy! Look for love in everything you do, both for yourself and others.

Questions: How often do you allow yourself to feel overwhelming emotion, or do you repress what you feel?

Affirmation: "I surrender and let love flow to me and through me."

Task: Allow yourself to feel whatever emotion comes up today. Do not repress anything.

Two of Cups

"This idea of shared humanity and the connections that we make with one another—that's what, in fact, makes life worth living."

~Clint Smith

Keywords: Connection, truce, attraction, friendship, equality, partnership, harmony, mutual trust

Meaning: This is a card of union, of two people coming together—whether it's in love, friendship, partnership, or a union of some description. There is often a deep spiritual or almost soulmate indication and a feeling of mutual respect and harmony. A deepening bond and progression in an existing relationship takes things to the next stage. See another person's point of view by walking in their shoes. Look for connections in your life.

Question: Do you let the people in your most important relationships know how much they mean to you?

Affirmation: "I always honor my relationships."

Task: Send a gift or random text to someone special today.

Three of Cups

"There are no strangers here.
Only friends you haven't yet met."

~William Butler Yeats

Keywords: Celebration, party, support of friends, pleasure, social contact, emotional happiness and joy

Meaning: This is a card of celebration, of merriment, of "girlie" fun, of successful conclusions to projects. It is a card of good times with friends and family. Celebrate any special event where people come together and forget their differences. This is often a good sign of weddings and celebrations that involve lots of people just having fun! The Three of Cups asks that you appreciate your friends.

Question: Do you feel stressed and need to lighten up?

Affirmation: "I am embraced and welcomed by the Universe."

Task: Organize a fun night out with your friends, or a girlie night in with a bottle of wine and a movie. There does not need to be a reason to have fun . . . does there?

Four of Cups

*"Most of us go through life
not knowing what we want, but feeling
darned sure this isn't it."*

~Unknown

Keywords: Apathy, boredom, self-absorption, antisocial, can't be bothered, taking things for granted, unmotivated, stagnation, lacking emotional satisfaction

Meaning: This card can indicate boredom and discontent, feeling weary, fed up, or disinterested in events going on around you. You may be stuck in a rut leading to self-pity. You could feel like you need to find your passion again. This shows a mood of dissatisfaction and also of shutting out the rest of the world. Be careful you don't dismiss something out of hand or miss an opportunity due to apathy or having closed yourself down, feeling as if there is no meaning or purpose to life. The Four of Cups can also indicate taking things for granted and, therefore, not recognizing something of value, even though it may be right under your nose. This can be a person or something material.

Question: Do you trust yourself and your instincts?

Affirmation: "There are opportunities wherever I look."

Task: How about saying yes to every opportunity that comes your way today? See where it leads you.

Five of Cups

"Everyone can master a grief but he that has it."

~William Shakespeare

Keywords: Loss, bereavement, regret, sorrow, disappointment, sadness, grief, living in the past, abandonment, loneliness, emotional baggage

Meaning: This card can indicate a sense of sadness and loss where things may not have gone as you'd hoped, leaving you disappointed. You might be focusing on the negative or have a feeling of being emotionally let down by someone or a betrayal. There is great loss, trauma, distress, and possibly grief. It can indicate grief through bereavement or raw feelings and emotions when associated with relationship breakup. It might mean that you've let your emotions trap you into a victim mentality. Seek professional help if you are struggling with grief. There is always someone available to lend a listening ear.

Question: Do you focus on disappointments for ages?

Affirmation: "I let go of the past and move forward to the future."

Task: Today, notice when you begin to feel unhappy, and focus on something that makes you happy. Don't let yourself dwell on the unhappy feeling, and if you must, then allow yourself to feel it for an allocated time; then move on.

Six of Cups

"Nostalgia is when you want things to stay the same. I know so many people staying in the same place."

~Jeanne Moreau

Keywords: Innocence, childhood, nostalgia, something from the past, happy memories, past memories, home sickness

Meaning: Past influences, or people or places from the past, will feature or make a reappearance. Happy memories from childhood could occur. It can also be someone coming back into your life from the past who will stir emotions within you. Nostalgia is indicated, or longing for things that used to be. You may be focusing too much on the past, imagining things that were, or how you *thought* they were. You may be acting in an immature manner. Allowing the past to influence your present could be an issue. It's time to let go of the past. You may have moved to a different location and feel homesick.

Question: What memories or issues from the past are appearing in your current life?

Affirmation: "I always focus my attention and living in the present moment."

Task: When was the last time you were truly happy? What stopped that, and what can you do today to bring that feeling back?

Seven of Cups

*"Visualization is daydreaming
with a purpose."*

~Bo Bennett

Keywords: Wishful thinking, options, choices, daydreaming, castles in the sky, distraction, multiple possibilities, hallucinations

Meaning: This is the card of choices and wishes—lots of choices, each of which could bring satisfaction in their own way. Deciding what is important and what is not from the options available is the order of the day. You may, however, be distracted by the many options. There may be choices that may not be real, but a figment of your imagination. There may be a temptation to get carried away with your thoughts or build castles in the air. You could be feeling overwhelmed with all the choices available, and don't know what to do or feel afraid of making the wrong choice. Take a step back and look at the pros and cons of each option before you make your decision.

Questions: When did you last avoid making a decision from a choice of options? What was your excuse? How did that turn out?

Affirmation: "I invite guidance and clarity."

Task: What are your current daydreams? List at least seven and then decide which one you will step toward to bring it to reality?

Eight of Cups

Eight of Cups

"Sometimes you have to move on without certain people. If they're meant to be in your life, they'll catch up."

~Mandy Hale

Keywords: Traveling, self-discovery, leaving a bad situation, fatigue, tiredness, moving on, weariness, walking away, abandoning, no going back, leaving something through your choice

Meaning: This card indicates a situation in which you were emotionally invested but now have decided to call it a day and move on. There may be a sense of disillusionment for the energy already invested, but realizing it isn't taking you where you'd hoped. It may be time to abandon the path in search of a new direction. This is not an easy choice, and you may not know where you are going, but know that the situation is over and that you must walk away now, no matter how painful. This card suggests that great strength and courage are required right now for you to walk away from the situation. You gave it your all, but now the chains need to be broken. You no longer need to be linked to a difficult person or situation. It has served its purpose. As Elsa says in *Frozen*: "Let it go, let it go!"

Question: What relationships or values are draining your energy, that you need to move on from?

Affirmation: "Everything I desire in life is in front of me."

Task: Today, go somewhere new by yourself.

Nine of Cups

*"We all have our own life to pursue,
our own kind of dream to be weaving,
and we all have the power to make
wishes come true, as long as we
keep believing."*

~Louisa May Alcott

Keywords: Wishes fulfilled, emotional satisfaction, pleasure, abundance, emotional well-being, accomplishment, stability, overindulgence, happiness, high self-esteem, celebration of life, passion for living

Meaning: The Nine of Cups is a wish fulfilled, the wish card. There is abundance and good cheer in personal and professional life—just a good sense of well-being, feeling confident on every level, bringing a high level of self-esteem. You have made it through whatever was distressing you, and now is the time to sit back and enjoy the good times. You totally deserve it! Contentment, material success, happiness, and pure indulgence of all the senses are indicated! Do not allow yourself to measure yourself against what others have. Whatever is for you will not go by you. It will come to you at the right time.

Question: What would you like to manifest in your life?

Affirmation: "I welcome miracles and magic into my life."

Task: Go out and do something that makes you happy. It does not have to be anything big or extravagant (unless you want it to be!) . . . just something that makes your heart sing for joy.

Ten of Cups

"Family isn't always blood. It's the people in your life who want you in theirs. The ones who accept you for who you are. The ones who would do anything to see you smile, and who love you no matter what."

~Unknown

Keywords: Family, happiness, joy, peace, commitment, marriage, love, fun, celebrating with family and friends, happy ever after, blessings, luck, stability, security

Meaning: The Ten of Cups represents happy families. You have achieved family security and stability, which makes you feel both inner and outer peace. There is a feeling of being emotionally fulfilled, especially in matters of the heart. This card can indicate a very happy and long-lasting marriage full of love and respect. It could be that you have come to the end of a project in which you were emotionally invested, and it makes you proud to have achieved what you did. You are advised to carry on with what you are doing, and do not get too complacent or start taking for granted what you have.

Question: What does family mean to you?

Affirmation: "I am grateful for every member of my family and friends who are also my family."

Task: Today, take a moment to look at what you have in your life. Appreciate your family and tell them that you do, as not everyone is lucky enough to have family.

Page of Cups

"Even though you're growing up, you should never stop having fun."

~Nina Dobrev

Keywords: Messages, emotional, intuitive, intimate, surprise, creativity, birth, pregnancy, new project, inner child, happy news, beauty, romantic proposals, crush on someone, a dreamer

Meaning: The Page of Cups is the bearer of messages and may indicate news or messages of an emotional nature—not just about love and romance, but news that will be felt on an emotional level beyond that. There could be an unexpected opportunity coming your way that will make you very happy. It could also indicate a thoughtful, caring, gentle, sensitive child who feels things deeply. It can indicate a Water sign person (Scorpio, Cancer, or Pisces) and may bring news of a birth or pregnancy, or creative ideas. This card could also indicate a very new relationship full of fun and surprises.

Questions: When was the last time you "took a chill pill" and had some pure and unadulterated fun? Why did you stop?

Affirmation: "My inner child is free and open to explore that part of me that loves to have fun."

Task: Take some time out and do something creative—maybe read a book on poetry, sign up for an art class, or even spend some time with a young child, letting your inner child out with them. Have fun! Paint, draw, dance, or play on the swings!

Knight of Cups

"Someday my prince will come."
~Snow White

Keywords: Romantic, imaginative, sensitive, vision, on a mission, emotional, loving, caring, proposal of marriage, being swept off your feet, gentle, creative, peaceful, listening to your heart, confident of your feelings, passionate yet tender

Meaning: This is a person who is dreamy, romantic, sensitive, and highly emotional when presenting love and friendship. There may be an offer of marriage, or of a date if you're single. This card can indicate moving forward in a way beneficial to your emotional happiness. It suggests an idealistic person, who may belong to Water signs of Scorpio, Pisces, or Cancer. The card could suggest a time to follow your heart to see where it takes you. Knights are about action, so instead of dreaming, get up and do what your heart desires. Maybe there are certain feelings you are repressing, too scared to show them . . . this card says to be like the knight and just express what is in your heart. Do not hold back your emotions.

Questions: Do you express yourself fully to people around you, even the ones that you are close to? If not, what holds you back?

Affirmation: "I stand up for myself and tell people how I feel."

Task: Tell someone how you really feel . . . something you have wanted to talk about but have been too scared to do so.

Queen of Cups

"The hand that rocks the cradle is the hand that rules the world."

~H. W. Beecher

Keywords: Loving, kindhearted, intuitive, psychic, spiritual, emotional understanding, compassionate, artistic, nurturing, caring, romantic, empathetic, faithful, loyal, peace, healer, mother

Meaning: You are required to look at a situation with compassion and understanding. Look for the good and positive. Listen to your intuition and be aware of it when making any decisions. This card indicates a mature female who may be a Scorpio, Cancer, or Pisces, who will be or is supportive and caring and can offer you advice and guidance. You may be feeling quite emotional and sensitive and keeping your problems to yourself. Find someone to share them with. Learn to trust your intuition. You may be an introvert who is highly sensitive to the chaos of the outside world. This is someone who loves children deeply. This person is an amazing mother.

Question: Which part of the attributes of the Queen do I need to implement into my life?

Affirmation: "I truly love myself and am emotionally secure."

Task: Go out into nature and admire the stunning beauty there is in this world. View what you see through the lens of your feelings. How do they make you feel?

King of Cups

"When you react, you let others control you. When you respond, you are in control."

~Bohdi Sanders

Keywords: Mature male, wise, calm, diplomatic, caring, tolerant, considerate, thoughtful, sensitive, peacekeeper, tolerant, teacher, honest, integrity, faithful, spiritual, affectionate

Meaning: This card is about someone who is easygoing and gentle, gets along with most people, and tends not to rock the boat. The King of Cups has or needs to develop the traits of compassion, kindness, and wisdom and is not very strong due to thinking emotionally, which can lead to not being truthful—as in not wanting to hurt anyone's feelings. The Cup King is a dreamer coming up with ideas, is highly creative, and may be a perfectionist. This person could be a male from the Water signs of Scorpio, Cancer, or Pisces and indicates being at peace with feelings and has no need to prove anything to anyone else. The King is not ruled by feelings but rules them. Maybe someone needs your shoulder to cry on and is looking for real, honest advice. No matter what is going on around you, no matter what buttons are being pressed, remain in control of your emotions and try to handle anything that comes your way in an emotionally balanced, mature way. Remember to maintain your dignity.

Questions: Do you tend to be aware of your feelings, or do you avoid them by keeping busy? What are you trying to avoid?

Affirmation: "I am worthy of all the compassion and kindness life can offer."

Task: Today, take the time to listen to someone. Actually listen, without the distraction of a mobile phone, tablet, TV, etc. What is the other person trying to say, and what advice can you give when you truly listen?

The Suit of Swords

Ace of Swords

"There's a beast in every man, and it stirs when you put a sword in his hand."

~Jorah Mormont

Ace of Swords

Keywords: Intuition, communication, premonition, perceptivity, going within, hidden secrets, mental clarity, focus, new beginnings, success, truth, justice, decision, cutting to the core, willpower, assertiveness, sudden revelation

Meaning: The Ace of Swords is able to cut through any confusion with clarity and focus, asking you to think clearly and with the head rather than with emotions and the heart. New beginnings or new ideas will require mental focus. Renewed willpower will develop where you were lacking before. Use your will and force in a situation, as well as honesty, and stand up for yourself. Legal matters will be to your benefit. This card may indicate the cutting away of old beliefs and ways of doing things. It also may be time to implement any new ideas you have been harboring. The beginning of something new could take place. Take charge of your life and be the ruler of your world!

Questions: Do you feel in control of your personal power, or do you feel as if it requires a boost?

Affirmation: "Each and every day my willpower becomes stronger."

Task: Take action on something you have been avoiding for fear of failure. Use all your energy in taking the first step, instead of focusing that energy on your fears.

Two of Swords

"Indecision is a virus that can run through an army and destroy its will to win or even to survive."

~Wendell Mayes

Keywords: Indecision, stalemate, blocked emotions, denial, avoidance, not wanting to see the truth, confusion, worry, stress, painful decisions, closed heat, in between, choices

Meaning: There is a blockage of the mind, and you may not be able to see clearly. If you choose to remain oblivious, as if you cannot see it, then it does not exist. This can also indicate confusion or not having all the information at hand to make a decision. This is a card of indecision and not knowing which way to turn, having stress and worry due to the situation. Denying something that is obvious, you have deliberately closed your eyes. It may indicate communication blocks with another or even choosing between two people.

Questions: What decision are you not wanting to make? Why?

Affirmation: "I have confidence in my decisions."

Task: Be decisive about something that you need to decide. Instead of procrastinating, just pick one option and see where it goes.

Three of Swords

"I know this transformation is painful, but you're not falling apart; you're just falling into something different, with a new capacity to be beautiful."

~William C. Hannan

Keywords: Heartbreak, loneliness, betrayal, grief, loss, separation, sorrow, trauma, upsets, conflict, sadness, tears, despondency, divorce, being cheated on

Meaning: This card indicates a quarrel or heartbreak that is causing immense pain and grief. Someone has betrayed you and stuck a sword in your heart, someone you never thought would. It may indicate a cheating partner. Alternately, it could be a literal heart attack. There are lots of emotions just now, and you may not be able to see clearly due to intense grief. You are distracted and completely overwhelmed with emotion and cannot think clearly. Although it looks bad, this card indicates that from this heartache, a new you will emerge who is wiser. There is a lesson within this situation. Allow yourself to grieve, and do not repress. The heart is much stronger than you think.

Question: Are you still harboring pain from the people who hurt you in the past?

Affirmation: "I am forgiving, loving, gentle, and kind, and life loves me."

Task: Seek help from a professional if you are having difficulty in letting go and forgiving someone who hurt you in the past.

Four of Swords

Four of Swords

"The goal of life is to make your heartbeat match the beat of the universe, to match your nature with Nature."

~Joseph Campbell

Keywords: Rest, contemplation, recuperation, respite, withdrawal, consolidation, solitude, time-out, mental exhaustion, sanctuary, illness, hospitalization, retreat, recharging your batteries

Meaning: Rest and recuperation is the message from this card. You may have been feeling mentally exhausted and needing to take some time out to rest, to gather your strength. You need to be alone and have some withdrawal time. Relax and sleep on whatever is giving you mental stress, and who knows, the answers may come to you when you "sleep on it." This card can also indicate a recovery from illness, where you need to rest if you have been sick. Maybe you feel as if you have been fighting the world—it's time to lay down your swords just for a while; otherwise you will not have the strength to fight the rest of the war.

Question: When was the last time you felt true inner peace?

Affirmation: "I am calm and relaxed in every situation."

Task: If you can, spend some time alone today, meditate to release tension in your body, or maybe even treat yourself to a day at the spa—by yourself. Anything that helps you relax and just be.

 Five of Swords

"Every time you see someone as less than you, question it."

~Byron Katie

Keywords: Selfishness, discord, dishonor, regrets, underhandedness, hidden agenda, deceit, hollow victory, defeat, deception, abuse, bullying, loss, lies, negative people

Meaning: There is conflict or victory but at someone else's expense. Arguments, hostility, and clique mentality are indicated. People try to take advantage of others by underhanded means through deceit, theft, or other hidden agendas. Someone is not being honest in their dealings— maybe they are only communicating half the message due to their own selfish interest. Do not take things for granted as someone else may have their eyes on those things if you take yours off. Doing something under intimidation or bullying is possible. Maybe you are with someone who is a bully or selfish and always has to have his/her own way at your expense. The swords could also mean that there is a situation that is controlling you.

Question: What is so important to you that you feel the need to prove everyone else wrong?

Affirmation: "I follow my own path of happiness."

Task: Today, apologize to someone you have wronged but have let pride stop you from saying you are sorry.

Six of Swords

"Leave your burden behind, forget your troubles, sweep away your sadness, and let peace be with you."

~Ian Anthony

Keywords: Journey, moving forward, calmer times, recovery, travel over water, moving on, holidays, healing, mental stability, transitioning, ending of a difficult phase, light at end of tunnel

Meaning: You are moving away from difficult times, with the worst now behind you. Take away the lessons and go into the calmer time that is coming up. Life is going to be more settled now. You may also be feeling quite drained and tired after your tough time, so make sure you take time to recover. There is a sense of exhaustion, almost being "battle weary" as you transition from one situation to another. It may not have been what you wanted, but there was nothing you could have done—and although it may have resulted in emotional distress, the best thing is to move away, keeping in mind the lessons you learned from the experience. Allow yourself to grieve the loss but keep moving forward. You may actually be taking a journey over water. This is a time of making great progress. You are moving from one frame of mind to another.

Questions: What is changing right now in your life? Are you allowing for a peaceful transition or are you fighting it?

Affirmation: "Today, I leave the past and create a new future."

Task: Consider taking a trip over water today, or book yourself a short holiday.

Seven of Swords

"When you're dealing with frauds and liars, listen more to what they don't say than what they do."

~DaShanne Stokes

Keywords: Deception, evasion, being careful, sneakiness, running away, dishonor, treachery, plotting and planning, escaping, lies, enemy within, theft, cheating, frenemy, cunning

Meaning: This card indicates acting in a way that is dishonorable or sneaky. Someone is trying to take something away from you in an underhanded manner or is avoiding a confrontation by running away from it. There could be a person who is a liar or is a "friend" (not really, but is masquerading as a friend), talking about you behind your back. Someone with suspect motives toward you or you toward another is possible. Infidelity could rise in a relationship. You might not be honest about your feelings, and cover up what you really feel. The card could also be asking you to use your wits to outsmart a situation or a dilemma you find yourself in.

Question: In what way are you deceiving yourself?

Affirmation: "Today, I let go of something negative in my life."

Task: If someone annoys you today, tell them—instead of talking about them behind their back to someone else.

Eight of Swords

*"Man is made by his belief.
As he believes, so he is."*

~Johann Wolfgang von Goethe

Keywords: Trapped by fear, restriction, constraints, confusion, powerless, limitations, obstacles, doubt, confinement, prison, depressed, paralyzed, stagnated, blocked, enslaved, helpless

Meaning: There is self-imposed restriction or the feeling of being trapped due to your own thinking. You could have been backed into a corner by someone else. The restrictions may be *in*ternal and not *ex*ternal. Is someone being trapped by a fear that is not real? You are able to free yourself from these bindings, but you are choosing not to. You may be giving away your personal power to someone else and letting someone else control you, thinking you have no other choice in a situation. You may believe you have no options and that you are stuck in a situation you cannot get out of—but you can if you let go of the belief that you can't. The situation is of your own making, but options are available if you choose to see them—change your perception!

Questions: Has an experience from your past made you feel worthless? What is keeping you stuck in that belief?

Affirmation: "I am a survivor, and I am worthy."

Task: Today, choose a belief that has kept you stuck and fearful. What belief would you like to replace it with, and what steps will you take today to live the new belief?

Nine of Swords

Nine of Swords

*"The key to change . . .
is to let go of fear."*

~Rosanne Cash

Keywords: Worry, guilt, anguish, stress, anxiety, fears, nightmares, grieving, despair, illness, distress, insomnia, ghosts from the past, unable to face situation, dark night of the soul, loneliness, terror, fears larger than what they are

Meaning: Worry and stress are keeping you awake at night. You are listening to the voices in your head, which are making the worries and fears even larger than what they are. Confront your fears as they are not as scary as you have imagined them to be. You may be feeling guilty about something that happened, and you are still stressing over it. You may be feeling overwhelmed, unable to cope or find a way out. Health issues may require hospital visits. Life may feel at an all-time low for you, and you do not know where to turn. This card may indicate a serious illness, which has you worried because you do not know how to cope.

Questions: What thoughts or nightmares tend to keep you awake? How real are those fears?

Affirmation: "I am confident and fearless."

Task: Pick something to do that really scares you. What would happen if you did it anyway? Write down what you would see, hear, and feel. Who is going to win—you or the imaginary fear?

Ten of Swords

"The trouble with life was that you didn't get a chance to practice before doing it for real."

~Terry Pratchett

Keywords: Victim mentality, being a martyr, stabbed in the back, disappointment, failure, feeling pinned down, misfortune, disillusioned, rock bottom, the end, death of a situation, closure, betrayal, chronic fatigue, defeat, end of the world, paralyzed, "woe is me" attitude

Meaning: A disappointing and painful ending that was not expected is indicated. Failure or collapse in the professional/personal life might also be issues. The ending of a cycle leads to a new opening, so all is not lost. Something has come to an end, causing emotional pain. Someone may have let you down; hence a feeling of being stabbed in the back. There may be a collapse from the stress and strain of your worries. You could be playing the role of a martyr by attention seeking. Perhaps you got caught out while running away from something, and it has now well and truly gotten you. If only you had faced whatever it was.

Question: Is there something that is making you feel paralyzed and unable to act?

Affirmation: "I refuse to be helpless. I claim my own power."

Task: If you are feeling tired and depleted, book yourself for a massage, or even some acupuncture, to help you let go of all the stress.

Page of Swords

"There's nothing that can help you understand your beliefs more than trying to explain them to an inquisitive child."

~Frank A. Clark

Page of Swords

Keywords: Truth, planning, ideas, communication, using the mind, honesty, logic, headstrong, aggressive, messages, thinker, just, quick witted, inquisitive, witty, mentally sharp, delayed news

Meaning: This card may indicate a delayed or disappointing message that was the opposite to what you were expecting. There are minor delays in a project. Be aware of gossip and troublemakers. There could be a child or someone from the Air signs (Gemini, Libra, or Aquarius) who is immature and has temper tantrums. Someone may be impatient and rash and not listening to others. You need to be patient at this time and not rush into anything. Maybe you are inside your head too much at the moment.

Questions: How do you react to feedback from people? Do you get defensive?

Affirmation: "I express my opinions easily to others."

Task: Allow yourself to lower your defenses and listen to what people have to say—with a rational head, instead of taking it personally.

Knight of Swords

*"Everyone is entitled to his own opinion,
but not his own facts."*

~Daniel Patrick Moynihan

Keywords: Direct, authoritative, logical, knowledgeable, chaotic, whirlwind, charge, rushing ahead, impulsive, headstrong, brainstorming, impatient, perfectionist, single minded, hero, soldier, talkative, direct

Meaning: This is an ambitious person. This card could indicate rushing headlong into something without thinking it through. A big change could suddenly unfold at an alarming speed—take charge quickly. Chaos can occur if a situation is not handled properly. A person from the Air signs (Gemini, Libra, or Aquarius) who is assertive but headstrong may be involved. Being focused and single minded, this person can still be quite impulsive and impatient to get things done. You may need to stand up for your rights at the moment if you feel you are not being heard.

Questions: Are you rushing through life by cramming lots of stuff into your day, or do you stop and take a break before starting the next task?

Affirmation: "I take action and get things accomplished."

Task: Take a break. Slow down today. Go for a long walk without your phone, etc., and just stop and take in your surroundings.

Queen of Swords

"Turn your wounds into wisdom."
~Oprah Winfrey

Keywords: Honest, astute, witty, experience, forthright, calm, swift action, decisive, perceptive, independent, shrewd, independent, integrity, organizer, divorced woman, sophisticated, chatty, self-disciplined, candid, self-reliant, discerning, mediator

Meaning: This queen may indicate an older woman of the Air signs (Gemini, Libra, or Aquarius), who may be single, widowed, or divorced—she may help you out with a problem. This card tells of someone who processes thoughts quickly in a situation and is strong willed and independent. There is a need for fair play and justice in a situation. A need to embrace your personal authority, strength, and power is indicated. You or someone else has a sharp wit. This queen is someone who has had to overcome a great deal in her life and now has the wisdom to pass on to you. She does not suffer fools gladly and will fight in your corner.

Questions: Do you stand up for what you believe in, no matter what others expect of you? Can you say no?

Affirmation: "I have everything I need to create my own opportunities."

Task: Today, say no to something you really do not want to do but usually do to please others.

King of Swords

*"But I am the real Strider, fortunately.
I am Aragorn, son of Arathorn, and if by
life or death I can save you, I will."*

~J. R. R. Tolkien

Keywords: Authority, logical, analytical, stern, detached, law, mental discipline, conversation, decisive, justice, calm, intellectual, articulate, ethical, wisdom, fair decisions, honest, efficient

Meaning: The King of Swords takes nonsense from no one and sees straight to the core of the matter. There is a need to develop a structure and routine in life. Legal issues may be surrounding you at the moment. You need to deal with matters in an honest and just way, without letting emotions get in the way. Be realistic and think with the head rather than the heart. This card indicates an intelligent, honest, rational, and logical male from the Air signs (Gemini, Libra, or Aquarius). It can represent a lawyer or someone in uniform where legal dealings are required. There could be a relationship where the connection is intellectual. There might be a stern boss. Lack of structure could be present.

Question: Do you find yourself judging others before you have a chance to know them?

Affirmation: "I consider all points of view without any judgment."

Task: Volunteer to organize and lead something in the workplace or within the community

The Suit of Wands

Ace of Wands

*"Enthusiasm is excitement
with inspiration, motivation,
and a pinch of creativity."*

~Bo Bennett

Keywords: Power, control, energy, will, direction, creativity, enthusiasm, courage, confidence, new career or project, fun, passion, vitality, spark, good news, fertility, birth, spontaneous

Meaning: A new job offer or a business opportunity could be in the works. An opportunity within an existing job, such as a promotion, is indicated. Do not wait for this opportunity as it will pass by as quickly as it arrived—strike while the iron is hot! A new project that will give opportunities for creativity, self-expression, development, power, initiative, and moving forward could apply. There might be a divine inspiration. A special invitation, via a call or email, may come your way, which will excite you. A new, passionate love affair or a new chapter in a relationship could be afoot. This may also indicate a pregnancy.

Questions: What arouses your passions and desires? How often do you take action to make them a reality?

Affirmation: "All my choices and decisions align me with my passions and desires."

Task: Do something creative—paint, draw, dance, anything that allows you to express your creativity.

Two of Wands

"Faith is taking the first step even when you don't see the whole staircase."

~Martin Luther King Jr.

Keywords: Travel, choice of two options, aspirations, personal power, boldness, planning, comparing, strategy, business partnership, restless, wanting adventure, leaving suddenly, detachment, withdrawing, waiting, exploring spiritual paths, vision

Meaning: This card indicates negotiating and collaborating with others, probably a partnership, most likely a business one. Someone could be deciding on a new career path. You could be making a choice between two options—both are okay but lead to different outcomes. Neither option is better than the other. See the bigger picture, instead of focusing on the details. You may be waiting for something to happen before you can move. You could be in a relationship that has become routine and dull, or you may be considering traveling together.

Question: Are you waiting for the right person, right job, right weight, etc., to make you happy?

Affirmation: "I trust myself and the choices I make."

Task: Break your routine. Take a different route to work today, or do your hair differently. If you have the same thing for lunch every day, try something new.

Three of Wands

*"Our actions are like ships,
which we may watch set out to sea
and not know when or with what
cargo they will return to port."*

~Iris Murdoch

Keywords: Foreign lands, growth, efforts paying off, happy with decisions, expansion, trading overseas, emigration, goal, direction, support, leadership, exploration, foresight, setting things in motion, long-distance relationship, freedom, success, adventure

Meaning: There is the opportunity for good progress in achieving a goal or goals. You have had a small success, but there is still a long way to go. Make sure you plan the future course to achieve goals. Support from others and seeing a long-term vision in what you are planning are indicated. Being a leader and going fearlessly where no one has gone before and having the courage to follow your heart is also a part of it. This card could indicate expanding your business overseas or travel involved with work. You may be planning an adventure in a far-off land, which may result in a holiday romance. Create your own life!

Question: Are you absolutely clear on what you want out of life?

Affirmation: "I savor new experiences"

Task: Do one thing today that gives you a sense of achievement.

Four of Wands

"We think there is endless time to live, but we never know which moment is last. So share, care, love, and celebrate every moment of life."

~Anonymous

Keywords: Celebration, freedom, excitement, stability, rewards, happiness, prosperity, achievement, gathering, parties, weddings, success, holidays, teamwork, harmony, peace, reunion, laying down roots

Meaning: A marriage or engagement celebration is indicated. Successful business partnerships and completion of projects relating to the home become important. You may have bought a new house, or you are finishing an existing redesign. You feel stability about the work already done, with the promise of more hard work required. Celebrate your achievement before you have to begin work again. Be very proud of all that you have achieved. You deserve it!

Question: When was the last time you had fun for no reason whatsoever?

Affirmation: "I celebrate life and all that it has to offer."

Task: Gather some friends and family together and just have a great night out. You are alive . . . is that not a reason to party? Celebrate life!

Five of Wands

Five of Wands

"We are never so much disposed to quarrel with others as when we are dissatisfied with ourselves."

~William Hazlitt

Keywords: Office politics, internal tension, competition, ambition, dishonor, conflict, disagreement, arguments, confusion, pettiness, bickering, assertive, aggressive, rows, frustration, competitiveness in a relationship

Meaning: This card could mean that you will be surrounded by bad-tempered people or aggression. It may be an indication of office politics, with people backbiting about you behind your back. This is temporary and can also indicate obstacles that other people have put in your way. You may be struggling internally with yourself . . . the sense of many critical voices telling you that you are not good enough, smart enough, etc. You may feel disconnected with the many parts of yourself that make you the unique person you are. Are you feeling that people are being uncooperative or defensive? Don't get drawn into the situation but deal with it calmly.

Question: Do you constantly compare yourself to others and feel you have to be better than them?

Affirmation: "I am in competition with no one."

Task: If you work in a team, today do something that someone else suggests, rather than doing it your way, even if you think you know a better way of doing it.

Six of Wands

"It is better to conquer yourself than to win a thousand battles. Then the victory is yours. It cannot be taken from you, not by angels or by demons, heaven or hell."

~Buddha

Keywords: Triumph, success, celebration, pride, acclaim, leadership, victory, fame, applause, in the spotlight, achievement, accolades, promotion, great news, leadership

Meaning: You have succeeded, and others are now applauding your success or victory. You have gone through a hard time and have triumphed against all odds—time to celebrate! This card may indicate a promotion, new job, exam success, or any type of award being bestowed upon you. You have worked very hard for this victory, so allow yourself to bask in the glory of it. The card could mean success in fighting your internal fears or demons.

Question: How often do you allow yourself to bask in your achievements?

Affirmation: "I always attract opportunities and success."

Task: Accept compliments today, without feeling embarrassed or being immodest. Acknowledge and accept other people's praise of you!

Seven of Wands

"Stand up for what you believe in, even if it means standing alone."

~Unknown

Keywords: Defiance, conviction, standing up for your beliefs, standing your ground, tenacity, resistance, assertiveness, defending, integrity, honor code, holding your own, strong willed, assertive, forceful, fighting your corner, fending off competitors who want your position, principles

Meaning: This card usually means standing up for what you believe in while feeling challenged by others. It's about having the strength of your convictions to stand your ground and to be able to defend your position. Stay true to your integrity at all times. An ongoing struggle, such as power struggles and having the courage to keep going even if you feel you are fighting alone, could be present. This card may mean not compromising, or settling, for second best. Fight for your relationship, if it is worth fighting for. You may not be like the others and may feel you are always having to fight to be who you are, as they want to make you like them.

Questions: How often do you stand up for what is right, or do you back down in the face of others' expectations?

Affirmation: "I am courageous and stand up for myself."

Task: Be assertive, stick up for what you believe in, and don't let others back you down.

Eight of Wands

"Speed is irrelevant if you are going in the wrong direction."

~Mahatma Gandhi

Keywords: Speed, travel overseas, things happening quickly, power, motion, conclusion, news, swiftness, movement, action, excitement, swept off your feet, momentum, freedom, progress

Meaning: This card indicates news and messages coming in very quickly. If something has been stuck, then expect it to suddenly start moving again. Whatever you do now will just take off and gain momentum really quickly—make sure you are prepared for it and don't get caught out. You may be about to travel overseas for a new opportunity or just for a vacation, where you may have a holiday romance that sweeps you off your feet. Make sure you take your time saying yes to any jobs you accept now, so that you do not end up taking on everything and have to juggle it all. Learn to say no to the things that are not relevant.

Questions: Is there something you are rushing into, and is it is making you feel overwhelmed? Are you getting carried away, or are you thinking things through?

Affirmation: "I am in control of my life and attitude."

Task: Do something today that you have been putting off or procrastinating. Just start it, and don't make any excuses.

Nine of Wands

"A hero is an ordinary individual who finds the strength to persevere and endure in spite of overwhelming obstacles."

~Christopher Reeve

Keywords: Battle weary, ongoing battle, wounded, persevering, last stand, defensive, stamina, holding on, battling, strength, will, determination, still standing, wary

Meaning: You may be exhausted fighting a battle—internal, external, or financial—and feel like you cannot go on. This card indicates that you are almost at the end of the battle and just need to draw the last bit of strength to carry on; dig deep to find the will that is there. You may need to pause a bit, reflect, and gather your strength before moving on again. Almost there but not quite . . . a final battle to go before the end, but the end is not as far away as you think—even though you are completely and utterly exhausted.

Questions: How often have you listened and acted on the voice in your head that tells you that you are not good enough "for . . . *x*"? Have you ever given up something you really wanted because of it?

Affirmation: "I am the hero of my own story."

Task: If you are struggling with something, seek advice from someone who has already been through it. Listen to them.

Ten of Wands

"It is easy to tell the toiler how best he can carry his pack. But no one can rate a burden's weight, until it has been on his back."

~Ella Wheeler Wilcox

Keywords: Overburdened, struggle, overextending, labor, taking on too much, responsibilities, weighed down, overwork, stress, delays, lost sight, taken for granted, cannot say no, burnout, exhaustion, under pressure

Meaning: This card indicates feeling overwhelmed, overworked, and exhausted. Have you taken on far more than you can possibly do and feel the struggle of it now? There is a risk of burnout if some of the load is not put aside. Maybe something that once gave you satisfaction is now a burden, and it's time to let it go. Maybe you cannot see where you are going and have lost sight of where you were heading due to overburdening yourself. You may be at the end of a project or job where you are lacking motivation to see it to the end and just wish it would be over. Consider delegating to others and keep only the essential for yourself, or start by saying NO.

Question: Are you tiring yourself out carrying the load for someone who is not pulling their weight?

Affirmation: "One task at a time is enough."

Task: Consider delegating today. If you have deadlines at work or at home, seek assistance to achieve them.

Page of Wands

"All our dreams can come true if we have the courage to pursue them."

~Walt Disney

Keywords: Aspirations, happy news, creativity, enthusiasm, courage, confidence, following a calling, a journey or adventure, high energy, ideas, passion, playful, active, original, gutsy, courage, fearless, extrovert, pushing boundaries

Meaning: The Page of Wands indicates happy news or messages of a creative nature, such as a new job or new opportunities that will get you excited and passionate. The news involves swift action to be taken, and it may come from someone linked to the Fire signs (Leo, Aries, or Sagittarius). Don't be afraid to take a risk at this time. Maybe you are thinking of starting something new, something that has you excited. Think big by having a vision and going for it. This card may also indicate a young child of the above signs who is playful and fearless. You could be heading for a new, passionate romance, full of excitement and adventure.

Question: What fires your passions?

Affirmation: "I am in the right place at the right time."

Task: Do something creative today. Start an art class, do pottery, redecorate, write a book, or even bake a cake!

Knight of Wands

Knight of Wands

*"Do not follow where the path may lead.
Go instead where there is no path
and leave a trail."*

~Ralph Waldo Emerson

Keywords: Daring, passionate, impetuous, adventure, risk taker, self-confidence, charming, activist, moving home, impulsiveness, show off, bragging, moving at speed, hasty, passionate, headstrong, energetic, bold, warrior, sudden

Meaning: This card could indicate a journey or adventure of some kind that involves lots of action and risk taking. This is the time to take action, but think things through and do not be hasty. You may have a house or work move that comes out of the blue with a sense of urgency. This can also involve a person from the Fire signs (Leo, Aries, or Sagittarius) who is a creative, fiery, passionate person entering your life. A passionate romance with someone from the Fire signs may sweep you off your feet, but may not be dependable as in "here one day and gone the next"! Someone is always on the move. You may be stuck in a rut, as this card is asking you to shake things up a bit, go exploring, and have an adventure. Anything to break the routine!

Question: When was the last time you were spontaneous?

Affirmation: "I enjoy exploring life's many possibilities."

Task: Try a new restaurant today instead of the same one you go to all the time. Or book a holiday in a place you have never been.

Queen of Wands

"And one day she discovered that she was fierce, and strong, and full of fire, and that not even she could hold herself back because her passion burned brighter than her fears."

~Mark Anthony

Keywords: Dynamic, powerful, energetic, superwoman, cheerful, passionate, confident, inspiring, self-assured, feisty, creative, visionary, fearless, ambitious, warrior, bold, optimistic, cheerful, sexy, efficient, independent

Meaning: The Queen of Wands may indicate a mature woman of the Fire signs (Leo, Sagittarius, or Aries) with the traits of being fiery, passionate, cheerful, and energetic. You may be taking on too much work and always keeping yourself busy, or, on the other hand, you may be spending too much time socializing. There might be an entrepreneurial woman who may help you. The need to be action oriented and resourceful is advised. You may need to cultivate independence. Stop caring about what others think about you. Have confidence in yourself.

Questions: Are you confident in who you are, or do you care about what other people think?

Affirmation: "I shine and sparkle wherever I go."

Task: If you are normally shy and retiring, be the opposite today. Allow yourself to be the center of attention for a change..

King of Wands

"Any fool with a bit of luck can find himself born into power. But earning it for yourself, that takes work."

~Lord Varys (*Game of Thrones*)

Keywords: Leader, inspiring, forceful, courageous, confident, charismatic, bold, noble, creative, dynamic, very romantic, earned respect, daring, go-getter, risk taker, visionary, entrepreneur, strong, powerful, larger-than-life character, generous, survivor

Meaning: You have the wisdom, experience, and energy to succeed at whatever it is you want to achieve now. You may need to consider taking a risk even though all the information is not at hand. You may be required to take on the role of fearless leader, and by leading with compassion and charisma, people will respect you. Trust in yourself, as you have what it takes to take charge of the situation. Be the boss! Be bold and fearless! Finish what your start. This card may indicates a dynamic man from the Fire signs (Aries, Leo, or Sagittarius).

Question: When was the last time you helped someone become excited and motivated?

Affirmation: "Motivation comes to me easily, and I successfully motivate others."

Task: Make a grand gesture today. Buy a box of chocolates for your team at work to let them know you appreciate them. Cook a dinner for your partner or friends for no reason at all.

The Suit of Pentacles

Ace of Pentacles

"Expect your every need to be met. Expect the answer to every problem; expect abundance on every level."

~Eileen Caddy

Keywords: New material beginnings, prosperity, trust, practicality, new venture, abundance possibility, investment, blessings, good fortune, new job, savings, security, stability, good health

Meaning: This is a card of new material beginnings. You may be starting a new job, which will bring you stability and financial security. It can also indicate the possibility of a new venture that will help increase abundance. A new source of money could be coming in, and prosperity. This card is about planting the seeds now so that they may grow and provide you with abundance. Things are not instant—you need to plan and wait with patience instead of expecting results straight away. It's now time to manifest what it is you desire; watch your thoughts, as what you think is what you will create. You may meet someone who provides you with a sense of stability and security.

Question: What kinds of seeds are you planting just now for the future?

Affirmation: "Money comes easily and effortlessly to me."

Task: Buy a lottery ticket today . . . you just never know what may happen!

Two of Pentacles

"When you gather up all the balls of life that you try to juggle, it is a very difficult thing to try to focus in on taking good care of yourself."

~Richard Simmons

Keywords: Juggling finances, flexibility, fun, balancing, multitasking, uncertainty, going around in circles, busyness, many plates spinning, adapting to change, financial decisions, money transfer, financial/material stress, not enough to go around

Meaning: You may be juggling with money and life. Maybe you do not know how to say no and, as a result, now have too many plates spinning in the air—and there is a danger of them crashing. There is the possibility of juggling finances with taking from one place to pay another. You may not be looking at how bad a situation is, and are going around in circles trying to fight reality. You could be trying very hard to make something work with the little you have. You may be giving out more than you are getting in. Know that this is temporary. You may need to find a work/life balance. A big purchase may be coming up, and you need to find the money for it. You may be working two jobs.

Question: What are the things you are currently juggling in order to keep life stable?

Affirmation: "Every area of my life is in perfect balance."

Task: Look at ways in which you can recycle what you have.

Three of Pentacles

"Success is no accident. It is hard work, perseverance, learning, studying, sacrifice, and most of all, love of what you are doing or learning to do."

~Pele

Keywords: Study, planning, strategizing, competence, new skill, learning, assessments, commitment, long-term plans, quality, hard work, building trade, architect, details, motivation, work ethic

Meaning: You may be learning new skills and enjoying the work that you do because you are good at it. You are being recognized for those skills. They build on your foundations for the future by practical planning and strategizing the work that you are doing. Work hard now to enjoy the fruits of labor later on. Perfect your skill by ongoing learning about your trade. Learn from your mistakes. There may be romance linked to work, or you could be working hard on an existing relationship. You may consider new spiritual practices.

Question: What aspects of your job do you enjoy and why?

Affirmation: "I feed my mind with new ideas and expand my level of knowledge."

Task: Sign up for a training course where you will be learning something to help advance you in your career or something that interests you.

Four of Pentacles

*"They measure their esteem
of each other by what each has,
and not by what each is."*

~Ralph Waldo Emerson

Keywords: Possessiveness, control, blocked, frugal, miserly, holding back, too cautious, saving, lack mentality, holding on, not letting go, withholding information, greed, saving up, financial protection, obsession, isolation, keeping to self, selfish

Meaning: This card indicates that you are secure, having what you need, but you are holding on to it and not wanting to share—whether that's money, possessions, or love. You may be afraid of not having enough, or that someone may take it away, so you are withholding. Relax, stop penny pinching; you have plenty to go around. By holding tight, you are blocking anything else coming in, as you are telling the Universe you don't have enough. This card may indicate control in a relationship where you are holding on to keep the person from leaving, or you could be holding back emotionally and not giving it your all. Perhaps you feel as if you are being controlled by another. Maybe you are holding on to a situation that no longer serves you, because it has given you security or you have a fear of letting go. This card can indicate saving for a big purchase. You may feel that the more possessions you have, the more people will like you. Why do you feel the need to be validated by others?

Question: Do you feel that no matter how much you achieve, it doesn't feel like it's enough?

Affirmation: "I give things away freely."

Task: Buy lunch/dinner for another person today.

Five of Pentacles

*"Loneliness and the feeling of being
unwanted is the most terrible poverty."*

~Mother Teresa

Keywords: Financial hardship or loss, needs, lack, ill health, rejection, feeling alone, poverty, recession, homeless, divorce, unemployment, scandal, alienation, negative circumstances

Meaning: Your circumstances may have changed, resulting in financial difficulties that are temporary. A large, unexpected bill may have come up that you had not budgeted for, and there is no money, or a debt is accumulating that you have no way of paying. There is a severe shortage of money. A feeling of being alone persists, as if there is no one to help you, but help is at hand if you can let others know you need assistance. Your pride may be stopping you from asking for help, as you may not want people to know your situation. Assistance is always there—you just need to ask, and you will see that you are not the only one in your situation. This card can indicate feeling abandoned or lonely in a relationship. There is a warning to live within your means, or you may end up paying the price. A single parent may be struggling to make ends meet for their family. Someone could be feeling emotionally, mentally, and spiritually destitute. You may have given too much of yourself to others and now are left running on empty. Stop and care for yourself.

Questions: Are you stuck in poverty consciousness? Why?

Affirmation: "I am open and receptive to all the wealth the Universe has to offer me."

Task: If you are struggling financially or in debt, connect with organizations that can help.

Six of Pentacles

"The wise man does not lay up his own treasures. The more he gives to others, the more he has for his own."

~Lao Tzu

Keywords: Charity, benevolence, sharing, giving too much, work/life balance, abundance, gifts, kindness, fairness, wealth, receiving, alms, compassion, loans, investors, windfall, assistance

Meaning: This card is about sharing your abundance with others, usually via charity or by helping someone who is in need. It may be that you offer money, or it may be your experience, abilities, or even your time with someone who needs it. Perhaps it is you who needs assistance and have to ask from another, such as a business loan. You may be about to repay a loan or debt, or someone owes you. You could be receiving a gift of money from another. This card can indicate that you are giving too much emotionally of yourself. Are you giving and getting nothing back in return because the person you are giving to is not appreciative of what you are offering? Is this leading to you feeling neglected and taken for granted? If your gifts are not being appreciated or are being taken for granted, then why do you continue? What are your reasons for continuing? That may be love, time, or money—it doesn't matter what it is, as giving and receiving should be balanced. This card is also about giving financial assistance, so if you are helping someone, then make sure you do not go into debt just to do so, as that will certainly not be of help to you!

Question: Whom do you share your resources, talents, and prosperity with?

Affirmation: "As I give, I receive."

Task: Donate to a charity of your choice today.

Seven of Pentacles

"What we plant in the soil of contemplation, we shall reap in the harvest of action."

~Meister Eckhart

Keywords: Profit, reward, harvesting, review, taking stock, appraisal, success, shares, pruning, results, trust fund, fulfilment, toil, hard work paying off, fruition, cultivation, nurturing

Meaning: You have worked a long time and very hard, and now it's time to harvest what you have sown. It is time to gather the fruits of your labor as you have planned, focused, and persevered to get to this point. It is time to pause, and take stock of where you are, and enjoy what you have earned. Look at where you've made mistakes and what you can do in the future to ensure that you do not do the same. This is a time of financial improvement, which can indicate loans, windfall, inheritance, or promotions, or it can come from investments you made awhile ago. Remain patient and do not try to rush things. Make sure you do step back; otherwise you run the risk of working for the sake of working without enjoying what you are doing. Appreciate what you have already created, and let it grow by itself now. Plan your next move. You may need to assess a relationship. Look at where it needs nurturing.

Question: How often do you stop to admire all the things your have achieved?

Affirmation: "My thoughts sow the seeds of what I want to manifest."

Task: Take a day off work. If you live near fields, go strawberry picking!

Eight of Pentacles

"Genius is one percent inspiration, ninety-nine percent perspiration."

~Thomas Edison

Keywords: Hard work, dedication, details, knowledge, skill, diligence, aspiration, patience, apprenticeship, learning, job satisfaction, perseverance, self-employment, expertise, scholarship

Meaning: This card indicates practicing your craft to become more accomplished, as well as honing skills and focusing on the job at hand. You love what you do, and it has stopped being a job—instead it is something that you enjoy. When you love what you do, then nothing feels like hard work. You do it because you enjoy it. You may be generating money from something that you love doing. Take your time to look through paperwork, making sure all details are correct. You don't want to be caught out later! This card can indicate a person who may be a perfectionist. You may be thinking of some new training to further yourself. It may be some mundane or routine training. Whatever it is, it will require a lot of hard work, and as long as you remain focused and dedicated to the task at hand, it's something that you will be proud of. There may be a new job in the cards, which will allow you to use all the experience and abilities at your disposal. It's something that will give you immense satisfaction and stability.

Question: How does the world around you benefit from what you do?

Affirmation: "I work with dedication and confidence."

Task: Do some DIY around your home.

Nine of Pentacles

Nine of Pentacles

"Happiness belongs to the self-sufficient."

~Aristotle

Keywords: Self-reliance, independence, refinement, luxury, material comforts, accomplishment, prosperity, financial stability, independent woman, abundance, indulgence, expensive tastes, status, elegance, finery, success

Meaning: This card represents success, financial stability, and security that you have earned by yourself. You may be a self-made entrepreneur who has expensive tastes and is prone to extravagance and a love of the finer things in life. Financial independence is indicated. You may be about to receive some money, or you may purchase something for yourself that could be considered a luxury item. Perhaps you are about to make a final payment on something that you owe. You may even have considered buying or renting a property on your own—your own private space—so you may set the ball rolling on that now. Be grateful for every second of the day. We may not have everything that we want, but we always have something that someone else is yearning for. So express your gratitude for all that is in your life, no matter how much or how little, as it's our perception that determines if we see too much or too little. You are so much richer than you can ever imagine. In fact, each day that we are alive is a gift, and if we can be grateful for that, then we are truly the richest people in the Universe.

Question: What are you grateful for in your life?

Affirmation: "I am self-reliant, creative, and persistent in all I do."

Task: Pamper yourself with a luxury face mask or bubble bath.

Ten of Pentacles

"No legacy is so rich as honesty."
~William Shakespeare

Keywords: Affluence, material stability, home life, success, inheritance, old money, family traditions, old-fashioned, settling down, heritage, windfall, thriving business, prosperity, pensions, wills, deeds, legacy, solid foundation

Meaning: This card indicates money coming to you through inheritance or from a family property sale. It represents financial abundance and a secure, stable family life. You have worked hard to achieve material stability, and it is now time to enjoy it. There could be a successful business. You may be in the process of securing or purchasing a home, new contract, new job, etc. Right now, it's as if everything you touch turns to gold! Long-term financial planning within a relationship could take place. You may hear about an inheritance, or you are advised to review any wills, trusts, or life insurances you have to ensure that everything is in correct order. It may be the time to invest in such policies. Are you in a position where you are able to help another who needs assistance? How can you help others to prosper? Now might be a good time for you to trace your ancestry. Consider getting a family tree done. It's time for you to slow down now, as your long-term vision has been realized.

Question: What lasting legacy do you want to leave to this world?

Affirmation: "I have everything I want and need."

Task: Make some memories with your family today and capture them on camera.

Page of Pentacles

"An investment in knowledge always pays the best interest."

~Benjamin Franklin

Keywords: Practical, trustworthy, messages about material matters, new project, planning, student, aiming high, new job, apprenticeship, hard worker, trustworthy, loyal, responsible, conservative, laying foundations

Meaning: This card usually brings good news or messages around finances, stability, and security. You need to decide if you want to accept what is being offered. It could be a new moneymaking venture, which will require lots of planning, practicality, time, and research to ensure it can be successful. It can also indicate that someone with the characteristics of the Earth signs of Taurus, Virgo, or Capricorn may cross your path and will be linked to money or resources. It is possible that you may get a place in a training course or secure a loan that you've applied for. Perhaps your boss suggests or sends you to a training course that you think is going to be boring—do not refuse it, as it will help you advance in the long run. Whatever you do now may help you with another opportunity further along. This is the time to begin planning for your future. You may be impatient and want it now, but the advice is to have patience and use this time to plan and prepare. You may be or about to be in a relationship where there is loyalty and stability. It may be that this person grounds you and may prove to be your rock in times of stress.

Question: How do you motivate yourself?

Affirmation: "Every day I am mastering new skills."

Task: Say yes to any opportunity that comes your way today.

Knight of Pentacles

*"Don't sweat the small stuff . . .
and it's all small stuff."*

~Richard Carlson

Keywords: Cautious, responsible, thorough, hardworking, realistic, practical, slow and steady, solid, trustworthy, consistent, methodical, disciplined, fixed, predictable, sincere, reliable

Meaning: This card indicates a situation finally moving along, even though it may be moving at a snail's pace. Slow-moving energy is being associated with work or a project. You may be frustrated that things are not moving as fast as you would like them to, but you need to let them go at their own pace. Rushing into anything could end up being quite expensive. Just go with the flow, and success is ensured. A person from the Earth signs of Taurus, Capricorn, or Virgo, who is hardworking and likes to create a financial nest egg no matter how long it takes, could be involved. They are usually dependable, honest, and trustworthy. It may be that you meet someone with these traits either in a romantic capacity or in a working relationship. Don't expect any fireworks with this Knight as they are quite happy just plodding along and getting things done. You may be feeling a bit disillusioned with life, and the advice is to use this time to cultivate optimism; use your setbacks as a tool for learning to change your mindset. As well as nurturing and growing our material possessions, we need to ensure that our minds are also nurtured and healthy.

Questions: In what area of your life are you struggling to demonstrate patience? What is the underlying reason for it?

Affirmation: "I have infinite patience."

Task: Do an activity today that requires time and patience.

Queen of Pentacles

"The heart of a mother is a deep abyss at the bottom of which you will always find forgiveness."

~Honore de Balzac

Keywords: Mature, homey, earthy, mother energy, organized, nurturing, charitable, supportive, generous, capable, practical, faithful, animal lover, capable, grounded, healer, protector

Meaning: Right now is the time for you to plan and be practical with work, personal life, and finances—maybe you need lists to keep on track of what needs to be done. Enjoy what you have just now. What you want will find a way to you. You may be someone who is homey and loves to be organized in the home environment, with maybe even a touch of OCD. There may be someone around you now who is needing your support and nurturing mother energy. You could be planning an indulgent weekend away with your partner. Women belonging to the Earth signs of Taurus, Capricorn, or Virgo may be involved. There is a need for you to look at how you experience and express the traits associated with this Queen: earthy, calm, grounded, wise, mature, good instincts, and trustworthy. You are advised to plan and not give too much sway to flighty ideas. Keep it real! Are you giving too much of yourself without receiving in return? Are you sacrificing your needs to nurture others? Maybe others have become too dependent on you, or you on them. Is it time to cut the apron strings?

Question: What self-care practices do you use?

Affirmation: "I take care of others by nurturing myself."

Task: Pick one outstanding household chore and complete it today.

King of Pentacles

"A good commander is benevolent and unconcerned with fame."

~Sun Tzu

Keywords: Mature male, supportive, enterprising, steady, adept, talented, wealth, reward, steadfast, astute, businessman, mentor, tenacious, patient, faithful, benevolent, ambitious, assets

Meaning: Your hard work has paid off, and you are financially secure. You may be required to play the role of provider to someone, whether that be personal or professional. It may be that a project appears that requires you to take on the role of a manager, using facts and figures instead of creativity for your decision-making. If you are having some financial issues, then you need to find a way to wisely make use of your resources; be realistic with what you have coming in and what is going out, or find someone who can help organize and budget. Draw up some sort of realistic plan of action. The need to prioritize is involved. You may be a bit of a hoarder, as you do not like wastage. This card can indicate an older man from the Earth signs of Taurus, Virgo, or Capricorn. You may meet this person at work, and he is a grounded, practical, conservative man working in finance or another related field. He will be steady, dependable, and faithful and will want to provide to ensure you have a secure and stable life. You may be thinking of purchasing some land or property as an investment for the future.

Questions: Have you set priorities for your life? What are they?

Affirmation: "I walk my path in this world with integrity to myself and others."

Task: If you have not done so already, make your will.

Acknowledgments

My husband, whose patience was very much tried by my obsession with creating this deck and his patience with me throughout the process.

My wonderful kids, Amber, Aaliyah, and Arran—because, well, they are my kids!

My fab in-laws (Tony and Barbara), for helping me with the wee boy (Arran) when I was busy trying to work, and he wanted to climb all over me!

Sue Ralston and Karen Wares, for their feedback on the cards as they were being created.

Ian Brander, for his unshakable faith in me and my creation and his words of encouragement during the creation, and for being there for me at all times when I have needed someone.

Chloe Esposito—for just being Chloe and my friend.

Sian Young, for being there for me always.

Hannah Frostick, for her enthusiasm and feedback on the images.

My editor (Dinah) and Schiffer Publishing, for taking on this project and bringing it to life.

Finally, to all you wonderful people who have bought the deck. Welcome to my world of Enchanted Dreams! Thank You all! xxx

About the Author/Artist

YASMEEN WESTWOOD always wished to be an artist but could not paint or draw. Then she came across Photoshop. Her passion for playing with images led to the creation of *The Tarot of Enchanted Dreams*. Yasmeen is a professional photographer who sees magic in both the people and landscapes she photographs. It is this magic that she has tried to depict in this Tarot deck. She holds a BSc (Hons) degree in biochemistry and MSc in immunopharmacology—both achieved in the UK. In a previous life, she worked in the oil and gas industry, training in health and safety and quality management. She is also trained in NLP, hypnotherapy, and life coaching, as well as being a Reiki master. She has combined all her experiences into this deck. But this is just the start as she is planning to create many more decks! Yasmeen lives in West Sussex with her husband, David, and their toddler, Arran.